The Snuff Takers Ephemeris®

THE JOURNAL OF FINE TOBACCO

Volume Six
Autumn 2012

© 2012, Lucien Publishing.

THE SNUFF TAKER'S EPHEMERIS is published quarterly by Lucien Publishing, Fayetteville NC. Volume Six, Spring 2012. Cost: 10.99/single volume; 43.96/per year. Address: PO Box 287, Spring Lake, NC 28390. www.STephemeris.com.

Advertising and distribution/bulk purchase queries: distribution@STephemeris.com.

ISBN-13: 978-0-9854781-1-7

ISBN-10: 098547811X

Contents

150–170: BONUS ISSUE: Monster Metal Megazine #138, August 1987

NEWS

BLACK TARMAC Xtra Strong Liquorice by: NICK AND JOHNNY

LIQUORICE

CRUSHED ICE Xtra Strong Mint by: NICK AND JOHNNY

MINT

White Heat strong White by: NICK AND JOHNNY

WHITE

RADICAL RED Xtra Strong Chili by: NICK AND JOHNNY

CHILI

BY: NICK AND JOHNNY

SWEDISH MATCH

SwedishSnus

WARNING: This product can cause gum disease and tooth loss.

On The Cover

Sir Philip Burne-Jones, *The Vampire*, 1897.

Burne-Jones (right) was a Baronet, son of painter Sir Edward Burne-Jones. This painting helped kick off the gothic vampire craze that has endured for the last 115 years.

Sir Philip used his then-lover Mrs. Patrick Campbell (bottom right) as the model for the vampress, suggestively straddling an unconscious man with a lustful gaze upon her face.

The painting immediately made waves on both sides of the Atlantic, and was soon exhibited all over the world. Author Rudyard Kipling saw the portrait, ran home, and wrote a poem based on the painting. Long out of print vampire books like *Varney the Vampire* and *Carmilla* were rushed back into print.

All of this helped to influence a struggling author named Bram Stoker, who was still working on a novel called *The Undead* that he had been writing, off and on, for a decade. After reading Kipling's poem and purchasing a print of Sir Philip's painting, Stoker decided to focus more on the main character of the book and throw in a heaping dose of vampirism. Thus, *The Undead* became *Dracula*, and it holds the record of being the best selling book of all time (after the Bible.)

Sir Philip continued painting for most of his life, but he never again achieved the success he scored with *The Vampire*. He died in 1926, in London, a beloved member of that city's high society.

"Mrs. Pat," or Mrs. Patrick Campbell as she was formally known, went on to become a famous stage actress, having a torrid (yet unconsummated) affair with director George Bernard Shaw. Once, while being described the lewd details of a back-alley orgy, she famously quipped "My dear, I don't care what they do, so long as they don't do it in the streets and frighten the horses." She died in Paris in 1940.

Every personality mentioned in this article had one thing in common beside their vampiric connection: they were each and every one a snuffer. STE

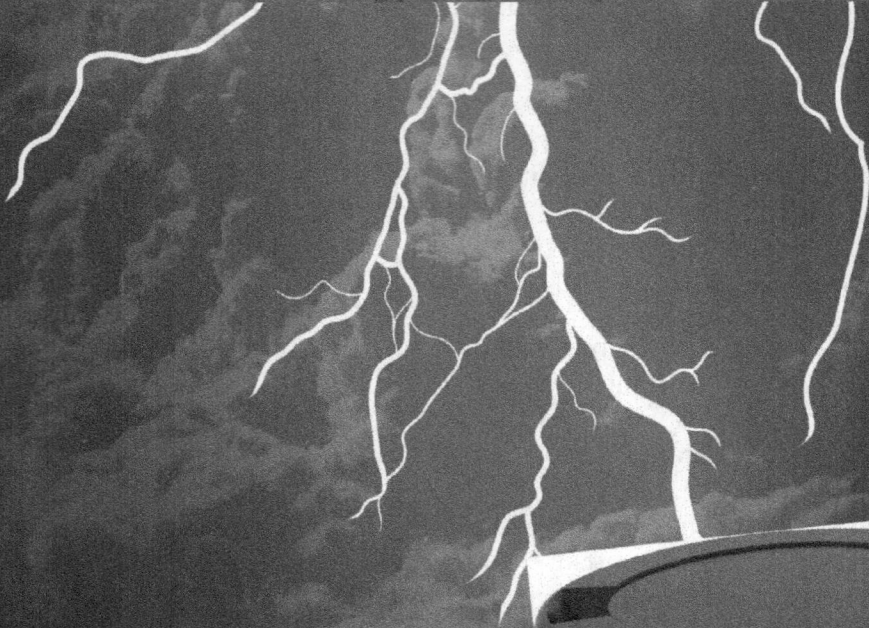

WARNING: Smokeless
tobacco is addictive

NOTE FROM THE PRESIDENT

We've had an absolute blast putting this issue together, from Motörhead to Bela Lugosi and all points in between. We haven't abandoned our original goal of making each issue better than the one that came before it, and we hope you'll agree that we've accomplished this with Volume VI.

If you'll allow me to be serious for a second, I wanted to mention that the elections are coming up soon and once again our freedom as adult Americans to enjoy tobacco hangs in the balance. I've thrown up a very simple scorecard to show you where the various candidates stand on tobacco rights:

	Increased taxes on tobacco use	Voted to restrict the ability for adults to purchase and use tobacco	Vowed to repeal federal tobacco taxes and put an end to unconstitutional anti-tobacco measures
Mitt Romney	√	√	
Barack Obama	√	√	

We at The Ephemeris aren't telling you which way to vote, or even to vote at all. But if you'd like an end to the unprecedented assault on our liberties as smokeless tobacco users over the last four years, you're going to have to look past the two "major" candidates. Clearly the modern two-party system is broken and a change is due. Choosing a third party candidate isn't "throwing your vote away", it's helping to shift the balance of power. If this wasn't true, the Democratic-Republican party would have never split into two factions and we'd all still be Federalists, Whigs or Tories. Otherwise, we're in for more of the same.

On a less-ominous note, we hope you enjoy the new "feel" of the Ephemeris. When we realized that 51% of our readership was female, and that 92% of our readership wanted to see pictures of these females, then a choice was made. Let us know what you think by dropping a line to **letters@STEphemeris.com**. (The Metal Magazine bonus "spreads" were a tongue-in-cheek parody, so don't expect much more of that. Unless...)

The poor man's Hugh Hefner,

RW Hubbard

Editorial

Change is constant.

I don't know who said it first. According to Wikiquote.org it was a guy named Heraclitus. It's been said by countless voices since. There have been several changes in the smokeless tobacco world since our last issue. In an effort to keep you up to date, I'll hit the big ones that affect my world.

Rob Jarzombek is back doing reviews for SnusCentral.org and Snustopia.com. Rob took a break from both sites and now that his duties at SnusOn.com have ended (under mysterious circumstances) and Rob and Larry Waters have kissed and made up (or whatever ageing hipsters call it when they work out their interpersonal issues), we can once again be blessed with Rob's unique style and accomplished taste buds telling me what I'm supposed to be tasting in a snus. Rob and Larry are both Snus Gurus for me personally and I'm very happy to see them working together again. I wouldn't be writing this today if not for those two guys. (Thank you, Gentlemen).

Next up is our friend **Rick Charles.** Rick has done more than any person I know to bring snus to the shelves of every B&M in the country. He still has a long way to go, but he's working on it. Until recently Rick was working with NorthernerUSA and handling 99% of the problems, phone calls, and trade shows by himself, even stuff that didn't fall under his job description. I do not know the details of the split between Rick and Northerner (mysterious circumstances again?) and I tried to get Rick to give me a snarky quote for this article, but he resisted temptation despite repeated attempts, which involved me calling him when I knew he was drunk. Rick has moved on though. He is now working for Kretek/Phillips & King. Doing mostly the same job, getting snus and snuff in every B&M store possible. We at the Ephemeris wish him the best of luck as always and will toss a public plea to get at least one store in Columbus Ohio to carry both.

One of my favorite homes away from home forums has changed ownership. **Snuffhouse.org** was recently purchased by **Dave Anderson of Mr.Snuff** from **Nigel McCarren,** maker of the Abraxas line of snuffs. Nigel has his hands full with snuff making and running a forum takes a lot of time and energy. I will let Nigel explain here in his own words: *"When Alex* [the original owner of Snuffhouse] *told me he was considering an offer from a German businessman to purchase the forum, I put my own bid in but, for me, it was just about keeping Snuffhouse in the hands of the community and my long-term intention was always to pass the site on when the time was right. I had been working with David Anderson on getting the Abraxas project off the ground and he was my natural choice to offer first refusal on the site, as I had come to really respect his approach to business. Snuffhouse is in safe hands."*

Now before there are any suspicions of Snuffhouse becoming an advertising tool for

MrSnuff... Dave is actually very hands off and the forum Moderators are given mostly free reign. From my point of view , being merely a member of the site, nothing has changed except the moderators are very much on the ball squelching trolls and posts that don't live up to the high standards that Snuffhouse is known for.

Speaking of Abraxas snuffs, there are new flavors on the way, likely already available as you read this. Well sort of new. **Abraxas Premium Batch** has a little brother known as **Abraxas Fin**, basically the same recipe just a finer grind. **Abraxas Connosieur Cerise** is back with an improved flavor and longer shelf life than the original lot. **Abraxas Dragun** has a cousin, **Dragun Menthol**. I haven't received samples yet, but am told it contains menthol and less chili pepper. As long as the menthol isn't overdone I bet it's a winner. At least in my house.

Roderick from **Toque** has announced that Toque branded snuff, limited flavors, and new flavors of **Silver Dollar** snuffs are now available to B&M stores in the U.S.A. I'm excited that I will soon be able to pick up real English style snuff at my local tobacconist. Thank you Roderick for the work and effort put into not only making the snuff in the first place, but going through the mountains of red tape to get the FDA to allow sales of Toque snuffs in B&M stores.

As you can see STE is still the same giant size it was last issue. This is also the biggest issue we've done so far, over 150 pages at the time of this writing (counting our included bonus issue, the *Monster Metal Megazine* from 1987. Let's see if this one gets past Canadian customs!) All for the same price as our last issue.

We're also, for the first time, taking subscriptions. U.S. customers will get free shipping, and there's some other goodies that we're working on in an effort to acquire as much money from you that we possibly can, while at the same time saving you as much cash as possible.

European readers will be happy to know that we're now distributed throughout Europe by Amazon and a few other online booksellers, all at roughly the same price as the American edition. But we still ship internationally from our site, so don't be afraid to order directly from us if you want to.

Sales of our digital edition are phenomenal, almost on par with the circulation of our print edition. I think the low cost (50% less than the printed edition), the portability and the full color of the e-zine version is helping to attract new readers that don't want to plunk down $10+ on a magazine they've never read. So at 4.99, there's no excuse to not sample our magazine- unless you're an absolute cheapskate that won't buy anything that costs more than 99 cents. (Note: you are a miserable miser and your family and friends all hate you.)

So change may be constant, but that doesn't neccesarily make it a bad thing. In fact, I positively like all the ones mentioned in this editorial. We hope you do too!

Mick Hellwig

Letters

STE,

I almost (notice I say "almost") stopped reading after issue 5 due to what I perceive as an anti-religious leaning that was apparent in this edition.

First, there's the swipe at Christians who oppose homosexuality when the anonymous author wrote that Christians that denounce being gay are in direct opposition to the Bible. This is a fallacy that we hear repeatedly today but it's wrong. **[The letter writer goes on to list a few passages from the Bible that condemn homosexuality]**. As you can see, God clearly looks down upon such vile practices.

[The author goes on for several paragraphs alleging that King James was not actually gay, but that all of these "rumors" were started by the Catholic Church, who wished for James to lose favor among the Puritans.]

Then there's the Bill Johnson article that is basically one big anti-Christian diatribe put forth and celebrated in our media by so-called "liberal theologians" that want God's laws to be altered to fit mankind's sins. It doesn't surprise me in the least to find out that he's been attending a Methodist church, as they've gone so far as to allow openly gay pastors to serve the pulpit.

I will keep reading your magazine if you hopefully veer away from the religious boundaries that you crossed in the last issue. I love God more than I love reading about tobacco, so please don't make me choose one over the other because your magazine will have to go.

Your brother in Christ,

P. Hopkins
Philadelphia, PA

Well, where to begin?

It was I (RW Hubbard) who wrote the piece on King James' alleged sexuality. Nowhere in the article do I say that the Bible doesn't condemn homosexuality. It quite clearly does (along with pretty much every other sin that man is wont to commit.) I merely pointed out that there are many Christians who use the original King James translation of the Bible to condemn gays, while King James was almost certainly gay himself. That's pretty ironic to me, which is why I pointed it out in the first place.

I'm not even going to attempt to dismantle your "King James wasn't gay" conspiracy theory. Believe what you will, but forgive me for thinking you a crackpot.

Bill Johnson has unfortunately been under the weather lately, so he wasn't able to personally reply to your letter. But since I've known him for the last thirty years I feel qualified speaking for him regarding this matter. Bill is not a liberal theologian in the least. From what I know of him, he's fairly fundamental in his beliefs and eschews many of the modern "spins" on Christianity that you've mentioned. Bill goes to a Methodist church because when you're in your eighties, you tend to not want to stray far from home. But I'm sure that if his church brought in an openly gay minister, Bill would find the extra energy to drive a further half a mile to the Free Will Baptist church up the street.

I personally don't care what your sexuality is, and neither does this magazine. The same can be said of your religious beliefs, political leanings and taste in food. I have my own opinions regarding those four subjects, but people buy this bookazine to read about tobacco and not to catch me making an ass of myself like Dan Savage.

I'm sorry you found Volume Five to be anti-Christian. I'm Christian myself. So are many of the staff writers. But it shouldn't matter what our faiths our, since this is a tobacco magazine. Period.

Your spy-for-the-pope / tool-of-the-marxists-brother in Christ, Rob Hubbard.

SHORT BUT SWEET

Hello,

I think the publication is truly excellent. I cherish and re-read my issues 1-4 very often. I greatly look forward to reading issue 5.

Tim Croft,
Louisville KY

SHORT BUT MEAN

You guys are dicks. The video on youtube [Ephemeris Boogaloo] just reinforced what I always thought about your publication.

Tom Green
via email

Geez, Tom. Ever since MTV cancelled your show and you split up with Drew Barrymore, you've been a real dick. Thanks for writing!

SHORT BUT STRANGE

Who was the hot guy at your booth at the Herocon in Charlotte? He signed my book but I can't make out his signature. I was the girl dressed up like Jessica Hamby from *True Blood*.

Kiki,
Hendersonville NC

I don't know who the "hot guy" was that you saw, but I was the only person from The Ephemeris there at our table at the Hero Con. I **do** remember you, simply because you were one of the six or seven people that actually bought a copy of our magazine!

PS: My wife says to never write me again.

LETTER OF THE MONTH

Friends at STE,

I have received my three volumes of The Snuff Taker's Ephemeris and must say I very much enjoy the material covered and your belief in free use of all tobacco products and the defense of those who use them. I myself have faced prejudice for using tobacco products on many occasions.

But I've seen the positive effects of tobacco use while I was deployed to Afghanistan in support of Operation Enduring Freedom. It has a calming effect on a man after a hard day's work fighting terror and having a few near death experiences, but I digress. Thank you for making this magazine, ephemeris, or publication, whatever you may call it- - I support you no matter what y'alls political views happen to be, because you support me: a tobacco user and a veteran.

Respectfully,
Specialist Paul Torres

Paul, we thank you from the bottom of our hearts for the time and sacrifice you and your fellow men and women of the Armed Forces have put in for our country, especially in these trying times.

Your letter was chosen because it caused us all to sit back and think for a bit about just how damn good we have it here at home, even though we whine about the trivial stuff. While our day is ruined because we lose internet for 2 hours, you and your buddies are sweating in the middle of a desert getting shot at by idiots. It truly puts things into perspective.

We get a lot of letters from military personnel stationed overseas, and it touches us to know that right now, somewhere, a group of GI's is passing around a copy of the STE and getting a few minutes of entertainment before stepping back into hell.

Thank you for your service, and enjoy the next four issues on us.

SEND US YOUR NEKKID PICS

To whom it may concern:

I read on your blog that you were hiring models to be in the magazine. Are you pulling locals or can anyone participate? If so, where do I send my portfolio?

Karen
Cincinnati, OH

Feel free to send us pictures of yourself or your friends reading our magazine or using smokeless tobacco. We'll begin running them here in the letters page. They can be sent to: **submissions@STephemeris.com.**

As for the actual pictorial models that we use in our photoshoots, we're only hiring out of the mid-North Carolina region, since that's where our photographer is based.

STE,

Is it true that they're trying to ban snus in Sweden? WTF?

Jeff,
Via Email

See Larry Waters' informative article this issue that pretty much sums up the entire stupid situation.

Hey guys,

What was the song that you used in that video for "Ephemeris Boogaloo"?

Kim
Via Youtube

It was Harry Manfredini's "disco" theme to Friday the 13th Part 3D. One of the greatest songs ever made, it went to #1 on Billboard's charts in Feb. 1983 and was covered by many prominent artists, including Juice Newton and Chuck Chillout. (Everything after that first sentence is a complete lie.)

And that pretty much wraps up this issue's letter column. Complaints, love letters, x-rated photographs, death threats and general mumblings can be sent to: Letters@STephemeris.com

Or if you want to kick it old school, send it to Letters, c/o STE: PO Box 287, Spring Lake, NC 28390.

STE

Ephemera!

... collecting all the news that's fit to reprint

Éire go crazy: Irish Senator loses his mind

Senator John Crown of Ireland recently celebrated the Parliamentary passage of his anti-smoking bill by calling for an outright ban on all tobacco use in the EU.

Crown was the mastermind behind the new Irish law that makes it a misdemeanor to smoke while your child is in the car with you. But like all tyrants, this measure wasn't enough to satisfy his thirst for control over the lives of his subjects. "We fell short in that we couldn't convince the entire EU to adopt this same ban, nor could we extend the ban to include other forms of tobacco."

We assume that the smoking ban was put in place to ensure that children weren't exposed to "deadly" secondhand smoke, but why would that same ban extend to smokeless tobacco? Will children develop some sort of cancer of the eyes if they witness their parents using snuff? Why do politicians continue to call smokeless tobacco bans "public health measures" instead of "do as we say because we know better than you" measures?

Vowing not to rest until all of the EU was completely tobacco-free, John Crown announced an initiative so bizarre that no other European politician since Hitler has attempted to enact it; to completely ban the manufacture, sale and use of tobacco products by the year 2025. "This is a time when the world is short of food. Imagine all that agricultural land being used to produce cancer-causing tobacco instead of being used to grow food."

Crown quite generously gives the tobacco industry thirteen years to adjust to the upheaval. "It will give the companies time to re-tool the machines to make something else." What that "something else" may be remains to be seen, but Crown offered a few suggestions, such as medicine. This makes perfect sense, as the millions of tobacco addicts out there will need expensive pharmaceutical items, like ineffective nicotine lozenges and re-appropriated anti-depressants that drive tobacco users to commit suicide.

And what *of* the poor, nicotine addicted users who will be left without their beloved tabacum plant? According to Crown, the 13 year transition period will "give the addicts due notice- if you're still alive in 10 to 15 years, you won't be able to get cigarettes legally."

Conversely, Senator John Crown has called for the legalization of Heroin and other narcotics to help "clean the streets" of junkies and criminals. Yes, you read that correctly: In John Crown's fantasy world, the average Heroin addict can go get a prescription for smack, but the nicotine addict will just have to "cope" with the change. Where's the IRA when you need them?

RI Governor vetoes "tough" law that punishes underage tobacco users

6/21/12- Rhode Island Governor Lincoln Chafee, an Independent, vetoed a new law that would see underage tobacco users face possible jail time.

Under current RI statue, a minor found in possession of tobacco faces a penalty of either 30 hours of community service or 30 hours of classroom time in a tobacco-cessation course. The new law would have the minor completing both an extended community service duration as well as the cessation course. Repeat offenders could even face jail time depending on the circumstance.

Chafee said that thirty hours of tobacco cessation schooling was "overkill" for the average teenager. He also noted that the "real" problem was the fact that a minor somehow came into possession of tobacco in the first place.

Four Indian Provinces Ban Smokeless Tobacco

Mumbai- Maharashtra, along with three other provincial Indian states, has banned the sale and use of most forms of smokeless tobacco.

India's oral cancer rate is the highest in the world, according to the CDC. Almost all reported cases are directly attributed to tobacco use, either from smoking or chewing. Popular types of smokeless tobacco include Gul, Guthka, Chiani, Masheri and Pan Masala. While these varieties of smokeless tobacco are on average much more carcinogenic than their Western counterparts, they are still safer in comparison to Indian smoking tobacco (which remains legal).

This contradiction in policy has been hotly contested by India's Smokeless Tobacco Federation, a group comprised of the country's leading smokeless tobacco manufacturers. Sanjay Bechan, the group's director, was quick to point out that the ban was instigated under the guise of food safety, a maneuver that was explicitly outlawed with the passage of the Tobacco and Other Tobaccos Act of 2003. "What they're doing is totally unconstitutional. Tobacco is tobacco, food is food. [The 2003 Act] was passed specifically to protect the tobacco makers from such prohibition."

He also pointed out that once smokeless tobacco is banned, people will likely switch to more dangerous smoking tobacco. Indian "bidis" (a type of cigarette) and Shisha (hookah tobacco) have been found to contain about five times more tar than the average American cigarette. "Smoking is the major cause of mouth cancer, but they're trying to make it seem as though guthka is the cause of it all. And that's just not factual."

Though not explicitly named in the ban, dry nasal snuff may eventually come under the same scrutiny as its smokeless brethren. Earlier this year, a comprehensive study of Indian snuffers concluded that they are no more at risk of developing cancer or heart disease than a non-user of tobacco. This however hasn't deterred politicians from calling for higher prices and increased legislation for the relatively harmless dry snuff.

NYC Warning Sign Law Struck Down

New York City- A federal appeals court ruled on July 10th that Mayor Bloomberg's forced tobacco signage was illegal and that requiring retailers to display the graphic warning images (above) trumped the Federal government's authority as the sole regulator of anti-tobacco propaganda.

The 2009 law required all stores that sold tobacco to display the large signs directly at the point of sale. "It was ridiculous," said one merchant who refused to comply with the law, racking up several hundred dollars in fines. "I run a deli. Who the f*** wants to order a sandwich and then see this nasty shit hanging in their face at the register?"

Several business owners, along with three tobacco companies, challenged the decision and the Manhattan District Court sided with the retailers. Bloomberg appealed the decision, and lost again- this time on a Federal level. The fiasco has cost New York taxpayers millions of dollars.

In addition to attempting to supercede the 1965 Federal Cigarette Labeling and Advertising Act, the law was repealed on the grounds that it interfered with the right of free commerce. Others questioned whether the law infringed on the First Amendment. "This suit has always been about who has the authority to regulate the content of cigarette warnings," Philip Morris said in a statement. "That is a power reserved to the federal government without interference or additional efforts by state and local authorities."

When pressed for comment, an agitated Mike Bloomberg began to sob uncontrollably. "Not... FAIR!" he screamed, kicking his desk repeatedly. He then threatened to hold his breath until he died, unless the courts repealed their decision. A spokeswoman for his office explained that Bloomberg had missed his nap that day, and was prone to fits of "rambunctiousness" when he became overly excited.

NEW STUFF:
All the fresh products that have launched since last issue

- **Samuel Gawith** Jubilee (SG)

- **Copenhagen** Southern Blend Longcut (USST)

- **Dragun** (Abraxas)

- **Paul Gotard** Vanilla, Aniseed Eucalyptus, Grape, Chocomint (PGP)

- **FUBAR Snafu** Plain & Medicated (Fubar)

- **Gawith Hoggarth Bulk** 22 varieties (GH)

- **Buzz** Bubblegum (Mr. Snuff)

- **Shikar** Guthka (Manikchand)

- **Talab** Guthka (Manikchand)

- **6 Photo** Motia (6 Photo)

- **Viking** Blonde (Viking)

- **Camel** Mint Snus (RJR)

- **Molen's Windmill Snuff*** Nutmeg, White Pepper Spice, Mixed Meat, Dutch Cookie Spice, Curry Spice, Cinammon Spice, Potpourri No.1 and 2, Chococreme, Chocomint, Mentholin, Choco (*re-releases) (De Kralingse)

- **Dean Swift** Wallflower, Specific, Rose, Lavender, Cinnamon, Carnation, Black Watch (WoS)

- **Wilson's** Natural, Sherry, Ice Licorice (WoS)

- **Gotland's** Summer Snus (Gotlandssnus AB)

- **Goteborg's Rapé** Lime, Lingon (formerly Goteborg's Rapé #2) (SMAB)

- **Thunder** Cool Mint, Cool Orange Extra Strong Portions, Wintergreen Longcut (v2)

- **Al Capone** Vanilla (Northerner)

- **DOS** Mint, Citrus (Northerner)

- **Catch** Spring Street Apple Cinnamon, Black Currant (SMAB)

- **Grinds** Tobacco-Free Coffee pouches: Mocha, Mint Chocolate, Cinammon Roll (GR)

- **Skruf Select** Halfcan, Yellow White and Blue Original (limited edition can design) (Skruf AB)

- **Jagarpris** and **Blue Ocean** Tobacco Cuts (AG)

- **General** Long Extra Strong, Long White Extra Strong (SMAB)

- **Grov** Motorhead (SMAB)

- **Lab Series 07** White Extra Strong (SMAB)

- **Granit** Strong White (F&L)

- **Olde Ving** (formerly Olde Viking) Snus (GJ)

- **Oden's** Cold, Extreme Vanilla (GJ)

- **Toque** (Six Flavors) (Toque)

- **Stok** (13 Varieties) (Stok)

- **Nick & Johnny** Tarmac (SM)

Cigarettes Losing Ground To Smokeless Tobacco

Reynolds American, who own the Camel brand (as well as the American Snuff line of products) announced a second quarter increase of 39% in overall sales. Continuing the trend from the last two years, cigarette sales reached a 6.7% decline while smokeless sales are up 10.7%. This increase in snuff and snus sales "more than makes up for [our] steadily declining cigarette market."

Though the increase in smokeless sales are directly attributed to category leader Camel Snus, sales are surprisingly on the rise for the company's stable of traditional dry snuffs. The report cited "solid earnings, steady volume growth" for its American Snuff line of "legacy" products, which include Garret, Dental and Tube Rose snuffs. Grizzly Moist Snuff also showed a healthy market earning, possibly due to the brand's new streamlined marketing push earlier this year.

Not to be outdone, Altria announced a 1.5% decline in the sale of their PMI Cigarettes (Marlboro, Parliament, Basic, etc) while their smokeless tobacco sales are up a whopping 7.6%. Unlike RJR, whose success in the smokeless category is directly attributable to snus while their moist snuff category remains somewhat stagnant, Altria's marketshare is based almost entirely on that company's USST moist snuff products such as Skoal and Copenhagen, while their Marlboro snus product fails to match the sales of rival Camel snus.

[Editor's note: maybe if Altria were to import the Swedish version of Marlboro snus, they wouldn't repeatedly take home the last-place trophy in the "Crappy American Snus" olympics.]

Director of the CDC Lies His Ass Off In Press Release

ATLANTA- Tom Frieden, director of the Center For Disease Control, issued a press statement full of lies and half-truths.

While overestimating the number of cigarette smoking deaths per year by including mythical "second hand smoking-related" deaths of non-smokers, he then goes on to make the absurd claim that "for every one person who dies from tobacco, 20 are disabled or disfigured or have a disease that is unpleasant, painful, expensive."

So where, exactly, are these approximately 300 million disabled, diseased and disfigured Americans Frieden cites as "proof" that "tobacco is the most dangerous drug in our society"? (Good news for crack and meth users: the drugs you abuse are much better for you than nicotine). Frieden cited no scientific studies, epidemiological research, guesswork or hearsay as the basis for his assertion. Quite simply, these "victims" don't exist and Frieden knows it.

Bill Godshall, director of CASAA, replied bluntly: "How can tobacco (or cigarette smoking) disable, disfigure or cause 350 million disabilities, disfigurements or diseases in the US in the past 40 years, or is the CDC now claiming that secondhand smoke has already disabled, disfigured or caused a disease in every nonsmoker in the US?

Besides, many CDC, NCI and US SG reports have consistently stated that cigarette smoking kills about one third of cigarette smokers. So even if smoking disabled, disfigured or caused a disease in the other two thirds of cigarette smokers, that would only account for twice the number of deaths caused by cigarettes. So who accounts for the other 90% of those who are disabled, disfigured or diseased by tobacco?"

Who indeed, Bill? Who indeed.

Swedish Match Introduces Catch Lids For North American Pouched Snuff Brands

The "Catch" Disposal lid (or, as it's known in Sweden, the "waste receptacle compartment") makes its American debut this summer.

Though the lid has been standard issue for Swedish snus cans for several years now, American companies have yet to "catch" on to the innovative design feature. The empty space above the main lid is meant to house used snus portions until the snuser is able to properly dispose of the spent portion in a trashcan. It was designed in an effort to clean up the streets of Stockholm, which are littered with spent portions. *(Editor's note: I can personally vouch for that statement. In my last visit to Sweden, I noticed that used snus portions are as common in the city streets as cigarette butts are in America.)*

Only time will tell if the Catch lid becomes standard issue on all pouched snuff products in America. Let's just hope they remain mysterious to dippers as they are for new snusers. Common statements we've overheard from noobs:

- "Why is there two lids? Is this can defective?"
- "I opened the lid but there's no snus in there."
- "Is this a POG?"
- "Is this like a collectible coin that you send in for free stuff?"
- "What is this, an ashtray?"
- "Is this a place to store pills or weed?"
- "That's stupid. If I need to get rid of a portion, I'll just throw it away."
- "We ain't got that stuff on American cans. Snus is for faggots."

FDA Makes Most Absurd Claim Yet Concerning Smokeless Tobacco

Obama-appointed Commissioner of the Food and Drug Administration Margaret Hamburg announced on July 12th that "To date, no tobacco products have been scientifically proven to reduce risk of tobacco-related disease, improve safety or cause less harm than other tobacco products,"- possibly the biggest lie yet to surface from her reckless and deadly regime.

Margaret A. Hamburg, MD
Commissioner of Food and Drugs

Yet another Chicago-based Obama crony that looks like a villain from an Austin Powers movie.

Hamburg then went on to pat herself on the back for accomplishing absolutely nothing in the field of tobacco harm reduction. Her absurd claims have been refuted by fact and statistic, yet you have to admire her singleminded pursuit of glory in the face of overwhelming evidence that she is a lying fraud. We invite you to read Mike Siegel's scathing rebuttal of Hamburg's nonsense at: **http://tobaccoanalysis.blogspot.com/2012/07/fda-commissioner-says-tobacco-act-is.html** .

Obituaries

- Renaissance man Gore Vidal died July 31st, aged 86. Writer, poet, political commentator and sometimes actor, he was known as "the Oscar Wilde of the 20th Century." His screenwriting credits were as diverse as *Ben-Hur* and *Caligula* and he penned the historical novels *Burr* and *Lincoln*. He sometimes wrote of tobacco, especially his early experiences as a five year old using Senate snuff:

I would wander on to the floor of the Senate, sit on my grandfather [Senator Thomas Gore's] desk if he wasn't ready to go, experiment with the snuff that was ritually allotted each senator; then I would lead him off the floor.

The first time I tried snuff, I attempted to eat it. This made me sick. The second time, I stuck it in my mouth and let it burn a hole into my tongue. I spit brown acid for twenty minutes. The third time, I sniffed it into my nose, and it made my eyes water and I sneezed. I thought, 'if this is what snuff does for you, why would anyone use it?' But by the twentieth and thirtieth time I used it, I didn't really care why anyone else used it, it made me feel warm.

Vidal died in Hollywood home from Pneumonia.

- Legendary Mexican singer Chavela Vargas died August 5th from respiratory failure. She was 93 years old. Vargas, famous for her groundbreaking musical routines, in which she skewered traditional gender roles by walking out on stage in men's clothing, spitting snuff juice into metal spitoons, and singing about the women she loved. She would sometimes don a fake moustache and sing with a foot-long cigar in her mouth.

Openly boasting of her lesbianism, she carried a pistol everywhere she went and dared anyone to call her a derogatory name. She once shot a policeman in the leg when he attempted to arrest her for drinking in public. She was never charged for the crime.

E-CIGARETTE NEWS

- Blu Cigs have recently been acquired by Lorillard for $135 million dollars. We can't wait to see what urban legends pop up about Newport e-cigs (see last issue).

- Swisher has launched a new line of E-Cigarettes and Cigars called "e-Swishers." The products are supposedly manufactured completely in the USA and will be available in a rechargeable kit as well as disposable form.

- NJOY brand e-Cigs have entered into a massive distribution deal that puts them in over 3,000 Circle K Convenience Stores across the country. Sales have been steadily increasing in the last year.

- Skycig UK, a Scottish E-Cig maker, announced a 1000% increase in business this year and plans to hire at least sixty new employees.

- RJ Reynolds intends to market a new line of harm reduction products under the brand name Vuse. Products will include e-cigs, dissolvables and lozenges.

- Green Smoke and V2 have joined forces to create SFATA, the Smoke Free Alternative Trade Association, an industry collective designed to inform consumers about the truth behind e-cigs and other harm reduction products while combating political ignorance and unfair legislation.

- blu Cigs has started a comprehensive retailer program designed to prevent underage sales of their e-cigs to minors.

- The UK *Vapers* e-cig forum has shut down due to legal threats from Jason Cropper, owner of Totally Wicked E-liquids. According to Vapers: *"Jason Cropper from Totally Wicked has announced on the forum an intention to sue for libel anyone who, in his opinion, unwarrantedly criticises Totally Wicked's products. We therefore advise all members to exercise caution when discussion Totally Wicked, their products or staff. We also remind members that they are responsible for the content of any postings they make."* Nevertheless, the site shut down a few days later. Hey Jason, your Gold Standard concentrate smells like cat piss. See you in court!

- Chinese company Dragonite (formerly Ruyan) sues ten e-cigarette companies in US for patent infringement of its "944 Patent" on cartomizers. (Communists have patent laws?)

- Phillip Morris intends on introducing Marlboro-branded "pseudo" e-cigs by 2017. PMI's speed in anticipating new alternative tobacco trends never fails to amaze us.

Mass-Backwards

Lies, Scandal and Debauchery in The Bay State

Massachusetts, the great state where freedom was born in America (and died there roughly about 1952) has been in the news so much lately with their anti-tobacco politics that we had to devote an entire column to it.

- Springfield and Pittsfield ban tobacco sales from pharmacies and grocery stores. This fits in with the 25 other Massachusetts cities that have placed similar bans.

- This pharmacy/grocery store ban is being pushed to become a state law by the State Public Health council, which voted unanimously to implement the prohibition but has had trouble finding House support for the legislation.

- In 2001, the Supreme Court struck down an unconstitutional Mass. law that forbade the display of tobacco advertisements anywhere within a store. Score one for the first amendment. Unfortunately, a new group of anti-tobacco zealots are pushing for a re-evaluation of the decision.

- Worcester Mass. Tried a similar "no store display" recently, which was quickly appealed and ruled unconstitutional by a Federal Judge.

- Harbor Towers, Boston's largest condominium resort, has gone completely smoke-free. New owners or residents will not be allowed to smoke within their own homes or anywhere on the property. The proposal was twice struck down in recent years, but passed this time with a very slim margin.

- The Dartmouth Board of Health is considering new tobacco prohibitions and taxes after hearing an impassioned speech full of lies from Judith Coykendall (see *Blackguard of the Month*, this issue).

- The towns of Saugus and Bedford are considering a new law that will require all cigars to be sold in factory-manufactured packages of four or more. Why? Nobody knows. Saugus is also trying to ban all tobacco use in the workplace, including smokeless tobacco and e-cigs.

- H.2452 is a bill introduced last year in the Mass. House that that would increase the cigarette tax from $2.51 to $3.26/pack, increase tax on cigars and smoking tobacco from 30% to 105% of the wholesale price, increase tax on smokeless tobacco from 90% to 135% of the wholesale price, and would allocate revenue to Tobacco Use Reduction and Prevention Fund. The bill was amended and is now in review (see next page.)

- The State legislature recently enacted a new law banning the purchase of tobacco products on government- issued debit cards, such as SSI and unemployment benefit direct-deposit debit cards. It looks like smokers on welfare will now have to hit an ATM up and physically withdraw the cash before buying tobacco.

- MA legislature's Joint Committee on Health Care Financing introduced H4291 as a substitute amendment to H2452 that would tax e-cigarette products and dissolvables by changing the definition of "smokeless tobacco" to include "any product containing, made, or derived from tobacco that is intended for human consumption, whether chewed, absorbed, dissolved, inhaled, snorted, sniffed, or ingested by any other means other than smoking, or any component, part, or accessory of a tobacco product." H4291, however, would exempt Big Pharma NRT tobacco products from any prohibition or excessive taxation.

- The Mass. State Senate amended and approved bill S2121 that would require the Commonwealth Care Health Insurance Program (Massachusetts' version of Obamacare) to provide, as benefits to all members, coverage for the cost of pharmaceutical NRT tobacco products (with an almost 97% failure rate), dangerous nicotine dependence drugs such as Chantix (also ineffective at smoke cessation, although it is pretty good for inducing suicide), and completely useless nicotine addiction psychological counseling and "support helplines."

- The town of Cohasset is attempting to ban public use of e-cigs, not for any health reasons, but because seeing someone vape "sets a bad example to children."

- Lynn, Mass., in addition to enacting one of the pharmacy tobacco bans in its township, is considering whether to cap the number of licenses to sell tobacco in their community. A new proposal would limit the number of authorized tobacco sellers to 180, thereby cutting the number of tobacco outlets in half. The measure is ostensibly to curb underage tobacco use, but how limiting the number of stores that sell an adults-only product only to adults will achieve this goal has yet to be explained. (*Editor's note: Will someone PLEASE think of the children?!?!*)

- Brookline residents vote 169-1 to increase minimum age for tobacco sales from 18 to 19 years, joining the towns of Needham and Belmont.

- Adams, Mass. Selectmen Skip Harrington urges Board of Health to ban e-cigarette sales, falsely stating that "They're purchased like candy. They are being sold like candy in this community," and "We need to take action in educating people and get them out of our community."

- The chain of 15 Pyramid Malls throughout New York and Massachusetts has prohibited its patrons from possessing or using tobacco (including snus and e-cigs) while in the mall. Exactly how they intend to implement this ban remains to be seen (security pat-downs at the entrances?)

Slash Stops Smoking, Switches to Shitty Snus

In a story broken by Anthony Haddad over at the Dr. Snus blog, it seems rocker Slash (Guns n' Roses, Velvet Revolver, Michael Jackson's "Black or White"- seriously) has recently stopped smoking his trademark three pack a day Marlboro Reds.

The guitarist, photographed here with Kevin Bacon (in costume for his role in the upcoming Tim Burton film *A Bunch of Weird Puppets and Johnny Depp*) extolled the virtues of snus in a recent interview with Charlotte, NC's Dirty Rock Nation.

Closer inspection of the photographs revealed a startling revelation, though: Slash appears to be using Camel SNUS Frost, an almost unfathomable product to be associated with someone supposedly as cool as Slash. Someone please send him Mikkey Dee's address immediately!

DrSnus.com

Family Dollar Bows to Pressure from Idiots

The chain of nationwide discount stores, Family Dollar, recently showed a lack of conviction by removing tobacco from all of their locations.

Family Dollar, responding to consumer desire for low-priced tobacco products, started carrying cigarettes and smokeless tobacco before The Legacy Foundation (the federally funded scumbags behind the "Truth" campaign) raised hell by sending in a petition signed by 16 anti-tobacco organizations. Within two weeks, all the tobacco was gone, leaving distributors holding the bag and confusing costumers in the process.

An employee at the Ray Road Family Dollar (Spring Lake, NC) that wished to remain anonymous pointed out the fallacy behind the move. "Look in this parking lot: there's a tobacco store, a Food Lion, and a gas station that all sell cigarettes. What was accomplished here?"

What was gained was another notch in the belt of the ailing Legacy foundation, which has lost millions of dollars in federal funding (as reported last issue). This affair smacks as a publicity move on their part to keep the Truth campaign in the news, rather than accomplish any real harm reduction.

Shame on the organizations that signed the petition, and shame on Family Dollar for going along with it. We urge our readers to shop at the Fred's chain instead, which has sold tobacco for 65 years and is generally cleaner inside than Family Dollar. Their prices are the same and they don't respond to frivolous criticism.

Smokeless Tobacco Now Safer Than Eggs

In another new study, eggs were found to be "2/3rds as dangerous" as cigarettes in the way they can damage the heart. Researchers say that egg eaters should limit their intake to no more than three per week.

According to the study, eating an egg every morning for breakfast has the same effect on the heart as smoking a half a pack of cigarettes. The report has been the subject of much controversy since its release.

But if the research pans out, and a carton of eggs is as dangerous as a carton of cigarettes, we expect the FDA to do the right thing and tax eggs to the point where premium brands cost about 40 bucks a carton. Oh, and they need giant warning labels on them. And sales to minors should be banned. And public consumption should be limited to very small "approved" areas.

Since smokeless tobacco is 98% safer than cigarettes, and eggs are only 33% safer, we expect President Obama to do the right thing and add snuff to the WIC and EBT programs, to ensure the health of our nation's children.

In all seriousness though, this study (even if it's flawed) adds another item to the list of Things That Are More Dangerous Than Snuff, like coffee, alcohol, prescription meds, smoking, obesity, carbonated drinks, the water we drink and the air we breath.

Hey America, see what happened in Australia? It's the same thing our President is fighting for

The so-called "plain packaging" law that the FDA is calling for (and Obama has agreed to pass) despite clear violation of the First Amendment has actually gone through in Australia.

The Australian law (almost identical to the FDA proposal in the US) makes all cigarette packages the same uniform design with a choice of four graphic images of throat/lung/oral cancer and the image of a dead little girl, ostensibly killed by secondhand smoke. The brand name appears in tiny 11 point type (smaller than the type you're reading right now) at the very bottom of the pack.

Something tells me that custom cigarette cases are going to make a comeback soon in Australia, just like violent crime did when they banned private ownership of firearms.

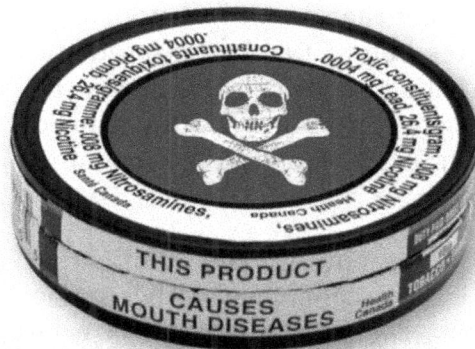

"I Couldn't believe what I was seeing"

McDonald's patrons describe the chilling outburst from a man high on "bath salts"

Nobody expected the horror that would unfold inside the Buda, TX McDonald's on June 6th, 2012. Andi McCormick and her two small children were eating their Happy Meals and watching the CNN scroll on the flat screen television display when it all began.

"I just had a flashback to seeing that negro man eating the other man's face on TV," she said, recalling the May 27th incident in Miami in which a man, apparently high on the designer drug known as "bath salts," stripped nude and began munching on a homeless person's face.

"Salting" incidents have been reported all over the country, mostly playing out the same way: The "salter" takes off his clothes and eats the faces of people that happen to be standing near him. This has led to a cannibalism epidemic in the US that "rivals even that of Africa," according to First Lady Michelle Obama.

The Texas McDonald's incident started off innocuously enough. A 27 year old man, later identified as Antoine Daddah, came to the counter and ordered a salad. After taking his seat, the patrons began noticing his bizarre behavior. "This guy was wearing a raincoat. I couldn't wrap my head around that one," claimed witness James Pharrel. Though it had been raining earlier that day, it had stopped at least 20 minutes before Daddah entered the restaurant. "That's just abnormal. I mean, the sun was starting to come out. Why did he need his raincoat? It made me watch him more closely."

Daddah then took out a black vial, later recovered at the scene, with the name "Abraxas" labeled on it. Police say that the people that make bath salts are often proud of their handiwork, and choose to put their "tag," or alias, on the container in which it's sold.

"It's a pride thing," Police Captain Jim McClusky told reporters. "This 'Abraxas' guy is getting his name out there. He wants people to know he makes some premium stuff, and so he flaunts it around with a label. Pretty soon there's a gang war between the Toques, The Fubars and The Abraxas guys over territory. A lot of innocent people are hurt in the process." McClusky says that he gets most of his "intel" from the television show *Breaking Bad.*

But what happened next shocked even the most jaded of witnesses. Daddah opened the container and began snorting the contents, as if it was cocaine. "I knew then that it was bath salts, because cocaine isn't brown," said bystander Sahara Santaseri. "Trust me, I know what cocaine looks like."

Daddah then stood up and began to remove his raincoat. "It was time for some action right then," recalled Percy Walker, Jr. "I know when they take them salts, they start stripping out they clothes. This dude was getting naked, and then he was probably going to start eating people. There won't no way in *hell* I was gonna let him eat my damn face."

Another patron noticed the clothes beginning to come off. Retired wrestling coach Doug Phelps said a "mental alarm" went off in his head, and he knew he needed to act fast. Using tactics he learned in his days as an elementary school wrestling coach, along with an almost

Daddah in the surveilance footage taken at McDonald's just minutes before his vicious attack

Doug Phelps, the man who took down Daddah. Police have dubbed him a "hero's hero."

encyclopedic knowledge of every episode of *Walker: Texas Ranger*, Phelps lunged at the confused Daddah, who was still attempting to remove his jacket.

"I could tell he was as high as a kite. He didn't know what was going on. He was saying 'why are you attacking me?' and 'get off of me, why is this happening?' Then when I put him in a chokehold, he bit my arm. That's when the situation reached critical and I knew that he was going to go for my face next."

Phelps slammed Daddah's head into the table repeatedly, trying to subdue him. "He was still trying to talk, even with all of his teeth knocked out. That's how whacked out he was."

The other patron, Percy Walker Jr., rushed in to help Phelps. "Dude was coughing up this weird mess, like brown stuff mixed with blood. It was pouring out of his nose like a fountain. I didn't know what the hell it was."

But Phelps did. "I knew this stuff could go airborne and infect the entire restaurant, so I had to stop it at the source." Phelps took off his Gold's Gym tanktop and held it tightly over Daddah's face and mouth.

"For a little guy, he was really resistant. I've seen this type of behavior before, when I coached kids on Ritalin. It puts them into "superman" mode where they feel nothing can hurt them. His legs were still kicking around so wildly that he dented the table that we were at. I know it took a lot of force to accomplish that."

But finally the wild thrashing stopped and Daddah slumped over, lifeless. The drugs he had taken had made him defecate in his pants during the struggle. By the time the police arrived at the scene, Daddah had expired. Police have ruled it a "suicide by drug overdose."

Andi McCormick says that Phelps' actions were a miracle. "I know that God was up there looking out for us that day, and he sent this man Doug Phelps to us to stop the man who was probably going to try and eat our faces."

Buda Mayor Sarah Mangham awarded Phelps with a key to the city and an expungement of his criminal record. "Now that I'm no longer registered as a sex offender, I can go back to teaching wrestling," Phelps said. "They took that right from me 12 years ago, and there's going to be hell to pay," said the modest hero.

STE

27

There is lots of news to report about Swedish Match this month running the gamut from exciting to unfortunate to infuriating. On the good side, we have two new and long awaited snuses to talk about; one from the **Lab Series** and one from **Nick and Johnny**. Swedish Match is also bringing back a popular **Catch Collection** flavor and a new can design is being unveiled for most of the **General** line.

On the sad side, we will be saying goodbye to one of the General snus products; at least until 2013 or perhaps forever.

On the legal front, Swedish Match Distribution is trying to enforce a labeling standard for the other snus manufacturer's brands that SM distribute in Sweden. (Even though the other manufacturers are competitors, Swedish Match still handles over 90% of the snus distribution throughout Sweden and Norway, including distribution of the rival brands). This is not sitting well with JTI Sweden and Skruf; not at all.

But first, the new products:

Swedish Match has been engaged in a complete remake of the **Nick and Johnny** snus line since 2010. It began with repacking existing N&J products and then moved on to new flavors with Crushed Ice Xtra Strong and Radical Red Xtra Strong Chili portion. Radical Red has even become part of my personal rotation as I enjoy it so much.

Now enter **Nick and Johnny Black Tarmac** Xtra Strong Licorice Portion Snus. Each can will contain 20 portions each weighing 1.1 grams, for a total weight of 22 grams per can. The nicotine level is approximately 15.4mg/portion. If Radical Red is any example, what Swedish Match calls 15.4mg/portion feels like 18mg to 20mg; at least to me.

The name of this snus is certainly worth commenting on. In English, it would refer to a stretch of asphalt which aircraft park on. Unless this snus was conceived of while Swedish Match snus designers were sitting on an airplane waiting to take off, I'm sure it has a completely different meaning in Swedish. Either way, it is a stand-out name which will which will certainly stick in consumers minds. Good job either way.

After stumbling onto **Romeo y Julieta** portion snus on my first trip to Sweden, I discovered I liked licorice snus. In my current rotation, the new Conny Andersson version of **Oden's Original Licorice** Portion snus is my favorite regular strength licorice snus at 9mg/g nicotine. I have high hopes for Nick and Johnny Black Tarmac filling my Xtra Strong licorice snus vacancy. It is expected to be available for sale Week 40.

Swedish Match has decided to redesign the can graphics for General Snus sold in Sweden and presumably through internet snus eStores. The changes will not affect the General Long Series or General ONYX (oh how we miss you!). The intent is to modernize and present a more unified appearance for the General brand. These changes will only apply to General snus round can products.

Back in February at the New York Snus Summit, we learned that **General Green Harvest** White Portion snus would cease production in June/July. We now know that distribution of Green Harvest will cease on Week 40.

General Green Harvest was a very popular snus but fell victim to its own success. Green Harvest was and is the only certified organic and pesticide-free snus on the market. Unfortunately, most tobacco farmers are more concerned with achieving maximum yield per acre, something that just isn't feasible today without using pesticides. Green Harvest was a blend of a half dozen or so pesticide free tobaccos. A large source was from Amish farmers in Pennsylvania.. so large, in fact, that Swedish Match pretty much cleaned them out. It will take time for the Amish tobacco farmers to regrow their tobacco stocks.

An unexpected setback for Green Harvest was the contracted Brazilian growers suddenly deciding to go back to using pesticides. Brazilian tobacco was also a critical component of General Green Harvest.

Originally, we were told Green Harvest would return next year once sufficient quantities of qualifying tobacco was available. This was before Conny Andersson and Swedish Match parted ways. Conny was THE man when it came to approving flavors, creating new blends and inspecting the tobacco that SM purchased. The latest announcement on Green Harvest states that it's "discontinued" which sounds a bit more permanent than "on hiatus." Time will tell.

General Green Harvest fans or those looking for a collectors item would be advised to purchase some Green Harvest backstock now, while a small quantity still exists.

Swedish Match **Lab Series** 07 Extra Strong White Portion snus was released less than two weeks ago. It is essentially the White Portion version of Lab Series 06 Extra Strong wet portion snus. For those new to snus, during the production process, wet/original/regular portions receive an extra few drops of water before they are canned. White portions do not, which makes the pouches appear white in color.

Neither method is better or worse than the other. The difference generally speaking is in the amount of time it takes for the portion to start running, the duration of the flavor, and the intensity of the flavor. I use and enjoy both types depending on the snus in question. Some, like Ettan, I like the white portion and the original portion. Others, like General Long Extra Strong, I prefer the wet portion over the white portion version. In the end, it's all up to your tastes.

Back on topic, the Lab Series is targeted towards the snus market in Norway although many in the US also enjoy it and the high nicotine levels it contains. A can of 07 contains 24 portions; 0.9 grams each. The nicotine level is rated at 16.2mg/portion. Like many snus consumers, I'm still waiting for the mysterious Lab Series 03 and 04; both of which numbers were skipped over. I'm sure there is a good historical reason in Sweden for this; that or marketing experienced a typing error when sending over the graphics requirements. I have no idea.

April's Catch Collection Lafayette Street mini portion snus is also making a comeback due to popular demand. It just became available again on August 27th.

And here's where it gets ugly...

There is a division of Swedish Match most Americans have no knowledge or reason to have knowledge of: Swedish Match Distribution (SMD). In Sweden, virtually all of the snus regardless of manufacturer is distributed to the retail stores in Sweden by SMD.

This has not pleased the other manufacturers, but Swedish Match effectively inherited distribution along with their brands when the last Swedish Tobacco Monopoly was broken up. Since that time, SMD has done everything it could to solidify and grow its distribution network.

If you look at snus chillers in any Swedish store (all snus sold in Sweden is refrigerated), you will usually find the Swedish Match products have prime display placement while other brands are relegated to the bottom of the chiller or even behind other brands. For years, the sales reps for the other manufacturers and SMD reps have played a game of 'moving the snus'. Kind of fun, actually.

A Taboca employee, for example, would move their products up to a prime position in the chiller. The next time the SMD rep visited, those cans would go back into obscurity. Snus manufacturers need SMD in the Swedish retail market; they don't like it, but can't do much about it.

As reported in a recent article in *di.se*, snus manufacturers JTI Sweden and Skruf have filed a complaint against snus giant Swedish Match with the Swedish Competition Authority. The reason is that Swedish Match wants to impose uniform signs in their snus fridges.

JTI Sweden (Camel, LD and Gustavus snus) and Skruf AB (Skruf, Knox snus) believe that Swedish Match is abusing its dominant position when the company requires other snus manufacturers to produce a label that follows a standardized style that Swedish Match has developed. If snus manufacturers do not do this, Swedish Match reserves the right to develop standardized labels and impose them on the other manufacturers.

Both JTI Sweden and Skruf correctly believe it will lead to a deterioration of the competitive situation for them and now wants the Swedish Competition Authority to put a stop to the label plans.

In the past, Swedish Match and their lawyers have not been shy about suing other snus manufacturers for using round snus cans, having stars on their snus cans, and intentionally designing labeling which could "confuse" the consumer into thinking these products were made by Swedish Match.

I certainly don't begrudge Swedish Match for trying. Any legal way to impede competitors has always been a part of good business. Look at the Apple vs. Samsung lawsuit which just concluded in California. Many of Apple's claims that they owned rectangles and touchscreens were laughable. As to the similarities in the appearance of the OS, blame Google for their design of Android, not Samsung who chose to use it. Regardless, Apple won.

Samsung can easily absorb the billion dollar USD fine. The future of Samsung wireless phones and tablets in the United States is suddenly very unclear however, and not a loss Samsung (or the Google Android OS) can absorb quite so easily.

Here is what I don't understand: Why aren't Swedish Match, JTI, Skruf/Imperial Tobacco, the Swedish Government, the Danish Government, and all the other snus manufacturers putting all their legal efforts into overturning the EU Snus Ban? Why aren't they fighting tooth and nail in Brussels? Cultural considerations aside, the measured/tepid response of "Here is our scientific data on snus. Please consider it when deliberating the Snus Ban" is just unacceptable.

It's time for diplomacy to end and the ruthless business tactics all involved have employed at one time or another to replace it. There was once a Swedish Empire. That didn't happen because Sweden nicely asked the other countries to surrender. Same for the Danish Empire. Screw the French; it was a fluke they had an empire in the first place and they ended up losing it in the end as usual.

It is clearly time for the politics of tobacco to end and the profits of Big Pharma to become irrelevant to the argument. It is time the Public Health take center stage based on true science and factual information. It's time to end business as usual; at least until the Snus Ban has been done away with. The clock is ticking towards the new EU TPD. STE

FROM THE ARCHIVES

Compressed Air
Magazine
August 1964

Compressed Air Magazine was a long-running periodical devoted to the joys of air compression. It's the type of magazine Hank Hill would have read if he wasn't crazy about propane and instead dug "air compressors and air compression accessories."

This 1964 issue featured a pretty good piece about the Continental Cigar factory, which produced the "Guinea Stinker" brands of cigars that Bela Lugosi (along with Frank Sinatra, Tony Bennet, Francis Ford Coppola, Mario Puzo and a host of other Italian-Americans) loved and smoked, and are still being manufactured today by the folks at Avanti.

The next time you're in the mood for a cigar and you don't want to break the bank, buy a pack of one of these ugly little cheroots and experience the bold, spicy flavor that tastes like it should cost more than it does. Anyway, since this was our Bela Lugosi tribute issue and he smoked the hell out of De Nobili and Parodi's, we figured we'd dust this one off and pull it out of the archives. Enjoy.

The automatic rolling machines at Continental Cigar Factory cut the leaf, deposit the filler, seal and trim the cigar. The entire process takes only a few seconds.

The Parodi cigars are then packed by hand 5 to a box, which is then put inside a larger carton for shipping.

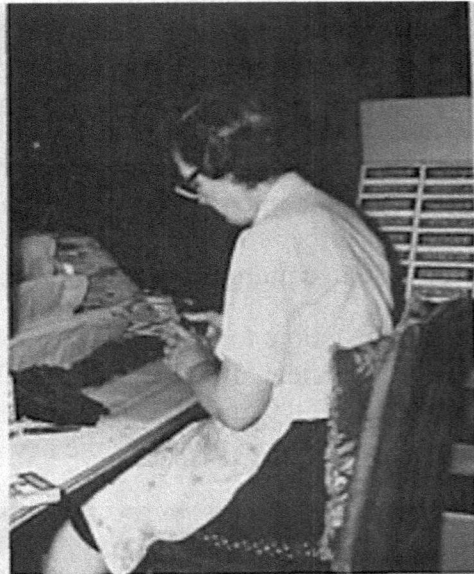

Making Cigars

"A good cigar is as great a comfort to a man as a good cry is to a woman."
Edward B. Lytton, 1836

Article by R.L. Moxey

Cigar manufacturing has advanced in recent months. Whether producing an American-type or an Italian brand such as Parodi, the industry has constantly improved its product. Likewise, production methods, since the primitive days when a few tobacco leaves were rolled in the palms of the hands, have been improved.

Parodi is the name given to the popular Italian cigar manufactured at Continental Cigar Company, Moonic PA. The operation at this 260-employee plant involve modern production methods, patient and exacting curing processes, and considerable use of compressed air. According to Continental's president, Anthony Suraci, "Air is more accurate than electricity. It allows us to modulate the various air controls whereas with electricity they are either on or off. This modulation is most important for the various pneumatically controlled curing processes. Air equipment has been added wherever possible." Suraci adds that there is very little maintenance necessary with air-operated apparatus.

At Continental, twenty different brands of cigars are manufactured in addition to the Parodi, including the De Nobili. A smell of tobacco mingled with an ammonia odor prevails in the plant. This is due to fermentation of tobacco filler. These odors are the result of the six month process of making a quality cigar.

The factory is almost completely air-conditioned, a 76 degree temperature being maintained. This is, of course, for the comfort of workers, but also for the conditioning of the tobacco. Humidity is also important and is maintained at 60% in the stemming, manufacturing, and cutting departments to keep tobacco from becoming too dry before the final cut.

The plant is set up to provide a complete circle of operation. Raw materials are received at, and finished cigars shipped from the same location. Materials received, such as tobacco containing barrels known as hogsheads, are put into a warehouse adjoining the receiving platform.

Conditioning

Proper conditioning of the tobacco is the first step in the cigar-making process at Continental. The Vacudyne Tobacco Conditioning unit is pneumatically controlled. Air at 100 psi is reduced by valves to 25 psi for this purpose. A hogshead containing filler tobacco is placed in the unit so that it temporarily mists the leaf. It is then necessary to remove the tightly packed tobacco leaves from the barrel. Hogsheads containing wrapper material bypass the Conditioner; they are opened as needed. Tobacco is misted in water and then placed in a sweat room. (The difference between wrapper tobacco and filler tobacco is that the former is full leaf without imperfections, while filler may have slight flaws in it such as holes or tears).

Steam Cycle

In the Vacudyne unit, moisture is introduced to the heated air and this makes the leaves fluffy and easier to handle. Dirt and waste is rinsed out after leaf removal to make way for the steam. The leaf goes back in the chamber and is met with a mixture of steam and air, which raises the temperature inside the unit to a high degree.

The Vacudyne is then evacuated a third time to bring this temperature down. The tobacco goes in for the last time, where a steam jet vacuum toasts the leaf to an even 110 degrees fahrenheit. Now that the tobacco is warm and moist, it can be handled easily without breaking or tearing it.

Sweat Room

The tobacco is then left to simmer in a vat of water for a few minutes to bring the heat level down to room temperature. From here the leaves are left overnight in a sweat chamber. Compressed air sends an even flow of moisture and heat throughout the room, keeping a uniform temperature of 110 degrees.

After a night in the sweat room, the tobacco is wheeled into the stemming department. Wrapper leaves, which have bypassed the Vacudyne system, have been rinsed off and spent a shorter period in the sweat room before being brought to the stemming department.

Stemming

The wrapper leaf is then placed on a machine that opens and spreads the leaf as wide as possible. A razor sharp aperture cuts the leaf evenly down the middle, leaving only the right portion and the left portion. The stem is discarded on the conveyer belt as the wrapper leaf heads further down to the curing area.

Filler tobacco is handstripped, however. The vein of the leaf is torn from its middle by hand. A good handstripper can remove up to 450 pounds of stem a day.

From here, the now cured and dry wrapper leaf goes straight to the tobacco production floor. Filler tobacco, however, is left in a pneumatically controlled fermenting room for a period of 2 weeks up to 6 months, depending on the brand.

Rolling

In the cigar manufacturing department, machines manufactured by American Machine & Foundry automatically roll the cigar-deposit filler into the wrapper, seal, then trim it. (Continental is the only manufacturer of Italian cigars in the USA that has an automatic rolling machine.)

The cigar rolling machine cuts the wrapper down to the required size. Size and shape of the cut are taken into consideration as one side of the cigar is more narrow than the other. This is the side that will be placed into the mouth. The blades that are used to cut the cigars are sharpened in-house by the company's machine shop, which handles about 70% of all machine repairs required by the factory.

To roll the cigar, the cut leaf is held on a plate by vacuum created by an exhaust fan. The exact amount of tobacco is deposited into a wrapper. An apron sweeps the cigar to the side where it is fully packed with filler before being trimmed. The cigar at this point is actually two cigars; it is later cut in half.

After each cigar passes visual examination, it is placed in a fermenting booth to further cure. It dries for about a week (or more, depending on whether the cigar is extra-fermented).

After this first maturation process, the cigars are placed into a hopper where they are cut in half. They are then bundled into larger stacks that are sent back to the fermenting booth. They are cured again for another two to three months in a 3-step process. The leaves become harder as they cure and the wrapper and the filler become amalgamated.

Packing

The Parodi brand is packed either in a two pack "King" sized package, or the normal five pack. The two packs are wrapped in a cardboard backer covered with Cellophane while the five pack is packaged in a small cardboard box that resembles a pack of playing cards. The two pack is assembled by machine while the five pack is assembled by hand. The packs are placed in larger boxes, crated, then shipped from the same loading dock that the hogsheads first arrived at six months earlier.

Compressors

The compressors used in the factory are Type 30 Ingersoll Rand units with 3hp motors. They have been operating 24 hours a day since being installed in 1960. Although the company only operates one shift, the humidification continues around the clock.

STE

How I Got My Boss Hooked On Snus

By Anthony Haddad

A few months back, the place I work at got a new boss. I heard that he was a smoker but never once saw him with a lit cigarette. Still, my snus friend at work and I decided that we should get him hooked on snus.

For a few months, whenever he'd come in to one of our offices, we'd offer him snus. But he never took us up on it.

Then a few weeks back, a VIP from out of town came in and the boss invited me, my snus friend, and another snuser at the office to dinner with him because we're probably the coolest people there.

That's not really saying much, but that doesn't make it untrue.

We went to this "cool" Japanese. The proof: there was a C-list actor at the table next to us. The servers brought out food irregularly, so I snused between dishes. When the subject of snus came up, I did my presentation about science and health risks and blah blah blah. The boss seemed skeptical and uninterested.

Then I told him about the trips General Snus has sent me on: Sweden, Chicago, New York, and the details of the recent trip to Las Vegas: the limos, the private jet, the 10,000-foot suite, the Dom Perignon.

Then he asked for some. Apparently douchebragging works on him. Philistine...

On Monday morning, the boss was in my office very early to get snus off me. I gave him a pack.

Then a few days later, I gave him another.

Then he ran out of snus and sent the following instant message:

"finished my last pouch in my last can. you f**kers got me hooked on this shit. now fix it!"

I gave him another. You don't want the boss in nicotine debt.

Eventually he made his way to a tobacco shop, and bought out the place.

Mission complete. STE

Bela Lugosi Lives*

(*... Despite what Bauhaus would have you believe.)

It's true, Bela Lugosi is alive and well and living in the hearts and minds of all who have come to admire the man and his work. Like the immortal Count Dracula he portrayed so many times, Lugosi will never meet the "true" death.

The purpose of this article is two-fold. First, if you're only familiar with Bela Lugosi as a dope-addict running around in a cape screaming "I VANT TO SUCK YOUR BLOOD!" (a'la Tim Burton's *Ed Wood* biopic), then you're in for a surprise. Lugosi was a gifted actor with many fine films to his credit. This article will help you learn more about the man and the characters he portrayed.

Secondly, and most importantly, very few writers, even Lugosi biographers and historians, bother to mention that Lugosi's number one passion in life (with the exception of acting) was tobacco. From snuff to cigars and everything in between, Lugosi was a true connoisseur of the brown leaf, and we've attempted to add a chapter to Bela's story that has been omitted for far too long.

So sit back and listen out for the children of the night... What tales they tell!

Born Béla Ferenc Dezső Blaskó on October 20th, 1882, to István and Paula Blaskó, Bela grew up in the town of Lugos. Lugos, located inside the area known as Transylvania was at that time part of the Austro-Hungarian Empire. (The town is now called Lugojsh and is located in present-day Romania.) Bela's father was a respected banker and he managed the family with a stern hand.

Bela, the youngest of the four Blasko children, was born with an innate dislike for authority. He despised the manner in which his father controlled the household, and would often leave church in the middle of service or ditch school to wander along the ancient caverns of the Trans-Carpathian mountains.

At age 14, his father literally dragged him to the Budapest trade school, so that he could further his education and hopefully become a lawyer or a banker, like his father. Bela achieved top marks in every subject except math, pretty much ruling out a profession in the banking profession. After a few months in Budapest, Bela ran away and became a miner. For the next five years, he spent most of his time underground mining for coal and developed a deep appreciation for darkness and solitude.

When he finally returned home to Transylvania, aged 19, he was saddened to learn that his father had been dead for three years. He decided to return to Budapest, this time to enter the Actor's Trade School in hopes of becoming a professional stage actor.

Bela spent a total of eight years there, as an understudy in summer stock performances. The first five years were the worst for him, due to his lack of formal education that often made him the butt of jokes of the other repertory of actors. He was the perennial "country bumpkin" in most plays at first. But he vowed to leave his humble

beginnings a distant memory, by educating himself as fully as possible. Most of his meager salary was spent on books, which he read voraciously until the day he died. It didn't matter what the subject was, Bela would finish a technical manual on airplane propellers and pick up a biography of Plato- sometimes reading up to six or seven books a day.

This self-transformation lead to Lugosi being considered a man of high-learning. He put on airs of aristocracy in the stage names he chose. Aristid Olt, one of his early aliases, literally translated as "The Aristocrat from the Olt River," the Hungarian equivalent of the Danube in Germany. Before he settled on "Lugosi" (meaning "from the town of Lugos") he often spelled it "Lugossy," to suggest a more upperclass Austrian heritage.

Now instead of comedic hillbilly roles, he was being picked for leading-man romantic dramas. Bela's star was beginning to rise just as the outbreak of war began. When Russia attempted to invade Hungary, Lugosi immediately enlisted in the army, even though actors were exempt from military service. Lugosi had exhibited the patriotism that he was known for all of his life, no matter the country he lived in.

Thankfully, his military career didn't last long. In less than two years, Lugosi had been shot in the chest, shoulder, legs and arm. He had suffered shrapnel damage to his back and neck. Four times he was put out of commission for his injuries, but once he was healed enough to walk, he was sent right back to the front lines. After the fifth serious injury that put him into a coma for a week, he decided that the military life wasn't for him and so he feigned insanity. The doctors all agreed that the concussion he suffered was enough to have permanently destroyed his brain functioning, and he was discharged honorably. As soon as he left the military hospital he caught a train back to

Budapest and began immediate rehearsals for the play that launched him into national superstardom. He was to play Christ in a play called *The Passion*.

The performances were highly successful. People openly wept, screamed and prayed as Lugosi languished on the cross, begging forgiveness for his torturers. Women fainted in the aisles. Before long, medical examiners were brought in to assist the audience. The play made headlines all throughout Europe.

Even then Lugosi was afraid of being typecast. He refused any more religious roles, and instead focused on comedic, suspenseful, heroic and dramatic parts that would demonstrate his versatility as an actor. In the process, he became a European sex symbol, "The Rudolph Valentino of Hungary", as the papers described him.

Other actors held him in high esteem, and he was chosen to head the Budapest Actor's Union due to his charismatic powers of persuasion. At that time in Hungary, the Theatre industry was controlled by the government. Actors were paid a mere pittance in comparison to the exorbitant salaries given to theatre owners, directors and film distributors. The Union pressed for better wages and a pension for actors, which the government refused to give into.

After appearing in over a dozen films over a two year period, Lugosi was approached by a man named Bela Kun, who presented himself to Lugosi as a Social Democrat. Kun persuaded Lugosi to align the actor's

Lugosi as Christ in 1916's The Passion.

Union with Kun's own revolutionary movement, who planned to hold a series of peaceful protests in front of government houses to fight the injustice against the working class, including actors like Bela. Lugosi agreed, not yet knowing what he had gotten himself into.

Around this same time, he married his first wife, Ilona Szmick. Szmick came from a prominent Budapest family who looked down upon Lugosi mainly for his career choice and low earnings. His father-in-law, however, was a loyal supporter of Kun's movement and was impressed that Lugosi was in such good graces with the increasingly notorious Bela Kun, and so allowed his daughter and new son-in-law to live on the second floor of the Szmick home.

The Actor's Union had finally succeeded in getting the wages that its members deserved, and there was much admiration for Lugosi in achieving this goal, though in truth he had done very little. Bela Kun, who had now declared himself a Communist, hadn't stopped with the Union struggles. He was now advocating violence against government officials and stirring up revolution amongst the working class, something that horrified Lugosi. He had only wanted fair wages for his union; he didn't want to overthrow a government!

Lugosi distanced himself from the entire movement, even dropping out of the Actor's Union which he had chartered. Kun had begun phase one of the "Red Terror" plot of 1919, which was to stage a coup and overthrow the government. Soon, to Lugosi's horror, his beloved Transylvania was a communist dictatorship. He began making plans to leave the country.

The Communist Overthrow was shortlived, though. The people reacted negatively to Kun's hired thugs who hunted down political enemies and had them murdered in the streets. The populace readily stepped back as Romania staged a counterrevolution and within four months, Kun and his communists were driven out of Budapest.

Lugosi was just as leery of the fascist counterrevolution as he was of the communist revolution. The Romanians soon began the two year "White Terror" movement that, as an ideological mixture of Fascist Italy and Nazi Germany, intended to rid Hungary of leftists, Bolsheviks, communists Gypsies, Jews, Homosexuals and other "enemies of the state." As an early supporter of Kun, Lugosi found his name on the top of the list of "aggressors" who were to be rounded up and executed.

Bela and his young wife fled to Vienna, Austria to escape the Romanians. While busy trying to find screen work there, he awoke one day to find his wife had left and gone back to Budapest at the behest of her parents. Her father, the diehard communist, had disowned Bela for abandoning the Red movement and so persuaded his daughter to leave the "coward" Lugosi. Bela was furious and heartbroken, and soon left Austria in favor of Germany in order to rid his mind of the previous year's series of events.

Lugosi threw himself into his work, making an astonishing 20 films in less than two years, along with the occasional stage performance. But for all his toil, he was broke. German actors were paid even less than in Hungary, and Lugosi knew he needed to get to America, where actors were paid more than politicians.

There was only one problem: he had no money to *go* to the US. Answering a newspaper ad that called for Hungarian ship hands, Lugosi talked his way into getting a job in the engine room of a merchant ship bound for New Orleans. The work was strenuous, but Lugosi didn't mind. He knew that once he got to America he could apply for citizenship and all of this hard labor would be behind him. There was only one problem- Bela almost didn't make it to New Orleans!

About three weeks into the voyage, one of the crewmen recognized Bela as the actor that once rallied for Kun the Communist. The Hungarian sailors were staunch Monarchists, and absolutely hated anyone that had anything to do with the Communist revolution. One crewman went to get his pistol while the other men held Lugosi down, the plan being to shoot him and throw him overboard. Lugosi managed to slip away and crawl into a nook above the engine compartment; a cramped, hot steel box no larger than a coffin. For four weeks, he hid there, and was brought milk and catfood by a man named Felix, his only friend on the ship. Bela urinated and defecated into a glass jar that was emptied out every evening by Felix.

When the ship finally reached port, Lugosi (in his own words) "ran like the devil" to the nearest policeman, proclaiming in his limited English that he was a political refugee and sought asylum from his captors. His story was quickly verified and within a few days had received his Green Card. Bela Lugosi, the Hungarian turned Romanian turned German (by way of Austria) was now Bela Lugosi, the American. He would remain a dedicated patriot for the rest of his life.

He traveled to Ellis Island for his naturalization papers (the process was finalized in 1931) and quickly ingrained himself into the small Hungarian actors community of New York affectionately called "The Nest". Stage roles were plenty, and he toured up the East coast performing mainly for Hungarian immigrant audiences. His first English speaking role was in Broadway's *The Red Poppy* in 1922. Still unable to speak fluent English, he learned his lines phonetically. This performance caught the attention of Fox Films, who cast him in

his first American film, 1923's *The Silent Command*.

Bela also married his second wife at this time, Ilona von Montagh. The two were inseparable, mainly because they were both jealous and obsessive over the other. They separated after two years, but kept in touch. In the fourth year, Illona went to Lugosi's flat in an effort to rekindle their marriage, but allegedly caught him in bed with the then "It Girl" Clara Bow. Divorce papers were written up the next week.

After a slew of minor roles in more American films, Lugosi's first big break came in 1927, when he was approached to play the title role in the stage version of *Dracula*. The play was a massive hit, running on Broadway for 261 consecutive days before going on an international tour. Lugosi would later be credited for playing the role of Dracula more than any other actor, though many are surprised to learn that he only played Dracula on film twice: 1931's *Dracula* and 1948's *Abbott and Costello meet Frankenstein*.

From the 1927 Stage Version of Dracula.

"DRACULA" *A Universal Production* MADE IN U.S.A.

I am... Dracula. I bid you... Welcome.

In 1929, Lugosi was married for four months to wealthy socialite widow Beatrice Weeks. Lugosi was apparently reluctant to marry her due to her alleged severe alcoholism. Taking a cue from Lugosi's previous ex-wife, she filed for divorce on the grounds that Lugosi was having an affair (a charge he always denied) but nevertheless, he didn't contest the divorce. Bela never "counted" his marriage to Weeks as a real marriage; when marrying his fifth wife Hope Lininger in 1955, he referred to her in the press as his fourth wife.

Even though Lugosi was known worldwide in the stage *Dracula*, he wasn't Universal's first choice to play him in the film adaptation. Conrad Veidt, Ian Keith, Paul Muni and Lon Chaney were all considered for the part, with Chaney allegedly contracted for the role before unexpectedly dropping dead at the last minute.

Carl Laemmle Jr, the film's producer, didn't care for Lugosi's performance after seeing him in a Los Angeles touring production of the play. Lugosi lobbied hard for the screen role, sending Laemmle newspaper reviews and write-ups that spoke positively of his acting ability. Finally, in an effort to get Lugosi off his back, Laemmle offered him the paltry sum of $500 per week, sans expenses, a salary far below the scale of the time. With such a cheap offer, he was sure Lugosi would walk away. To his surprise, Lugosi agreed immediately and began making arrangements to cancel his remaining stage performances.

The film's production was rocky, to say the least. For many of the cast members (including director Tod Browning) it was the first major sound film that they had worked on. Though Lugosi had been in a few soundies by that time, his performance was strictly rooted in the stage tradition, with dramatic, distorted body movement and slow, precise delivery ("I... bid you... *Welcome*" and "I never drink... *wine.*")

The special effects, also carried over from the stage version, are laughable by today's standards, but terrified audiences of the 1930s. The rubber bat on a string, the fog machine and cardboard sets are all noticeable today on Hi-def Blu-Ray, but the silver screens of 1931 masked many of the films imperfections.

Most of the moody, gothic feel of the film can be directly attributed to cinematographer Karl Freund. It's been estimated that he in fact directed at least 75% of the picture after director Tod Browning lost all interest in the film. Browning, supposedly despondent over not being able to collaborate with Lon Chaney, would rarely appear on set. According to Jack Foley, "He would show up, bark a few orders, then leave. Karl was responsible for the whole of that picture."

Regardless of the uneven direction of the movie, Dracula premiered at the Roxy Theater on Feb. 12, 1931 to rave reviews. Just like the stage version, people fainted in the aisles and had to be carried away in stretchers. Overnight, Lugosi's name was being repeated all over the country. He had now, finally, become the international star that he had always wanted to be.

Amidst this backdrop of stardom, Lugosi began courting his future wife, Lillian Arch, a woman nearly half his age. The daughter of Hungarian immigrants, the two fell in love instantly and dated for two years before eloping (against her father's wishes.)

Hot on the heels of *Dracula*, Universal offered him the lead role in *Frankenstein*. Lugosi screentested for the part (in full makeup) but in what may have been the biggest mistake in his career, he turned it down. "It's all grunting and groaning, and no dialogue. A mute could play the part." Instead, Boris Karloff, who had been toiling away in films for as long as Lugosi, got the part and became a star in the process.

Instead, Lugosi turned to more horror roles, but at least they had speaking parts. *White Zombie, Murders in the Rue Morgue, The Raven, Son of Frankenstein, The Black Cat, Isle of Lost Souls, Mark of the Vampire* and *The Invisible Ray* were all critically acclaimed horror films that he made during the 1930's.

In 1938, Bela's only child was born, Bela Lugosi, Jr. The younger Bela grew up to be a prominent California lawyer and goes by the professional name "Bela G. Lugosi" (G standing for *George*) to end confusion between he and his father.

By the 1940's, Bela realized he had been typecast. In the Players Directory, he took out a full page ad appealing directly to directors who thought him only fit for horror roles, a misconception that he called "an error." Instead of the "A" pictures he so desperately needed, he instead found himself on Hollywood's "Poverty Row," making such B movies as *Zombies on Broadway* and *The Return of the Ape Man.*

Incidentally, it was at this time that Lugosi began taking narcotics for a combination of problems. Every time it rained, his war wounds would flare up. On good days, he was nagged by a shooting sciatic pain. Finally, his doctors examined his limbs and determined that he was arthritic. Lugosi, the man who wouldn't even take an aspirin for a headache, was now being prescribed morphine and methadone, which he took every day. The medication didn't seem to affect his work, but the word got out that Bela was a "junkie" and he started having trouble finding work. His last "A" film ended up being 1948's *Abbot and Costello Meet Frankenstein*, his second and final screen appearance as Dracula.

Lugosi went back to the stage, touring in the odd summer stock play as well as an on again/off again five year revival of *Dracula*. He made numerous television appearances during this time, including a live skit on the Milton Berle show. When Berle began to ad-lib off of the script, Lugosi stuck to his written dialogue, which made him appear as though he had forgotten his lines. The incident embarrassed him badly enough that he vowed never to work in live television again. His only dramatic role for television was the 1949 episode of suspense that adapted Poe's *The Cask of Amontillado*.

The 1950's were even less kind to Lugosi. The best role he could muster was 1952's *Bela Lugosi Meets a Brooklyn Gorilla,* for which he was paid less than he was earning over twenty years earlier, pre-*Dracula* fame. The next year, he divorced his wife of 20 years because he suspected her of having an affair with Brian Donlevy, whom she worked with on the radio drama *Dangerous Assignment*. Although it's unclear whether Bela's paranoia was ever justified, Hope Lugosi eventually did marry Donlevy in 1966.

Hearing that one of his childhood idols was on the outs, amateur filmmaker Ed Wood soon knocked on Lugosi's door, offering him roles in several "idea" scripts that he had in mind. Ed would usually come up with a title and write the treatment around that. Such ideas were *The Ghoul Goes West, I Led Two Lives, Bride of the Atom-* even a proposed TV series to star Lugosi entitled *Dr. Acula*.

16 MYTHS ABOUT BELA LUGOSI

Almost since the time Lugosi achieved international stardom in 1931, a number of myths about the man have circulated as fact among Hollywood gossip columnists and biographers relying on 75 year old studio press kits. Listed below are just a few of them:

- **Lugosi was a hopeless heroin addict.** Lugosi never once tried heroin, although he was heavily dependent on morphine for several years. Lugosi suffered from crippling arthritis and pain from old war wounds in his legs, for which he was legitimately prescribed morphine. As the years went by and his tolerance grew higher, Lugosi's doctors switched him to Demerol, which was less effective than morphine. Lugosi had to take dangerous amounts of the narcotic, and his physician ultimately suggested that he check into a detox program to rid his body of opiates in order to try a new regimen of non-narcotic pain relief. After leaving the hospital, Lugosi never used narcotics again, but he was never able to find another drug to ease his pain the way morphine did. He chose to suffer in agony for the remainder of his life rather than be labeled a drug addict.

- **Lugosi was an alcoholic.** Lugosi actually rarely drank heavily until the last few years of his life. After giving up morphine, he found that the only way he could get to sleep at night was to drink himself to sleep, usually with Cutty Sark Scotch. Whether this makes him an alcoholic is open to debate, but he certainly wasn't the raging drunk portrayed in the *Ed Wood* movie. Prior to 1954, he only partook in the occasional social drink.

- **Lugosi hated cats, and was afraid of them.** This myth goes all the way back to a press interview done around the time of *Dracula*. In actuality, Lugosi loved cats and had adopted several strays before he died. He did prefer the company of canines to felines, however, and always kept a stable of dogs throughout his life.

- **Bela Lugosi hated Boris Karloff.** Karloff and Lugosi were great friends throughout life, and appeared in several films together. They would often send each other gifts that one would pick up with the other in mind, like smoking pipes or a box of cigars. While it was true that Lugosi always regretted passing up the lead in *Frankenstein*, the film that made Karloff a star, he never harbored any resentment towards Karloff personally. (In fact, the only negative thing that anyone had ever heard Lugosi say about Karloff was that he thought it was unprofessional for Boris to demand to break film production every day at noon for his afternoon tea.) The day before Lugosi died, while he was in a state of delirium, he rose suddenly from bed about 4:00 am and started getting dressed. His wife asked him where he was going, and Lugosi replied "Boris is waiting for me downstairs. I told him that I have a new pipe for him and he's there waiting for me." This was one of the last intelligible statements that he made before he passed away several hours later.

- **Lugosi died alone, penniless, and only six people went to his funeral.** This was probably the most unforgivable liberty taken by Tim Burton in the *Ed Wood* movie. At the time of his death, Lugosi was still married to his fifth wife, Hope, and lived a comfortable, unextravagant life in a middle class suburb of Los Angeles. Hundreds of friends, family members and movie industry professionals attended his funeral, and the mayor of Los Angeles declared August 18th "Bela Lugosi Day."

- **Lugosi cussed like a sailor.** Everyone that ever knew Lugosi personally claims that he never uttered a word of profanity in his life. Bela considered swearing to be indicative of lower class dereliction.

- **Lugosi was a womanizer.** Though he was divorced four times, only his third wife had ever accused him of adultery, an accusation that was probably not true.. But during his younger, pre-marriage days, Lugosi made no secret of his many relationships with famous women all over Europe. However, he considered marriage to be sacrosanct and claimed to have never suffered the weakness of infidelity. In fact, he divorced his third wife because *she* was allegedly having an affair with Brian Donlevy, whom she later married.

- *Lugosi wasn't a very good actor.* Though this is a matter of personal opinion, Lugosi's acting was unique and well liked by the critics of his day, as well as most modern film buffs. It's doubtful that he would have become an international star otherwise. But where some criticize his performances for being overly dramatic or as just plain overacting, one has to take into account the era that he started in. His loud, sometimes bizarre outbursts in dialogue came about from having performed on stage hundreds of times before ever appearing in a motion picture. And although he spoke English perfectly well, his accentuations were based on the Hungarian rhythm of speech, which resulted in sometimes off-kilter delivery. His physical "overacting" (exaggerated facial expressions, dramatic body movement) was very common for actors of his era who had made the transition from silent films to "talkies." While many of his peers eventually abandoned this acting method, Lugosi never strayed too far from it. This made his performances somewhat idiosyncratic with the rest of the actors in his later post-war films.

- *Lugosi once said "He's as gentle as a kitchen."* Ed Wood started this myth back in the 60's and it's persisted to this day. The story goes that while filming *The Bride of the Monster*, Lugosi's line was supposed to be "He's as gentle as a kitten." But Ed Wood said that Lugosi was unable to pronounce the word "kitten," so it came out sounding as though he said "kitchen." This was all complete lie, refuted by nearly everyone that worked on the picture. A home viewing of the film today reveals the truth; there is no "kitchen" to be heard.

- *Lugosi was a Communist.* Actually, Lugosi was what we would consider now a right-of-center conservative, who believed in capitalism, even when it didn't work out in his favor. In his early days, he was forced to leave Hungary because of union ties to Bela Kun, the Communist revolutionary. But his ties were superficial and once he learned of Kun's true intentions, Lugosi publicly distanced himself from the Communist party. It cost him his first wife, and very nearly his own life.

- *Bela's unique vocal delivery in* **Dracula** *was due to him learning the lines phonetically, as he hadn't yet mastered the English language.* Though this was true for a few of Lugosi's early plays, by 1931 he was speaking English as well as he ever would.

- *Bela died while reading an Ed Wood script called* **The Final Curtain**. Another Ed Wood-comprised fable, completely untrue.

- *Bela Lugosi requested to be buried in one of his Dracula capes.* Though he was in fact buried in his trademark cloak and signet ring, he had never requested anything of the sort. Lillian Lugosi and their son Bela Jr. decided on the arrangement, Bela Jr. stating that his father "probably would have wanted it that way."

- *Lugosi slept in coffins.* This one is semi-true; often while playing the stage role in *Dracula*, Lugosi would finish his rehearsals a few hours before showtime and would try to catch a nap. Usually he would climb into the prop coffin behind stage since it was the closest thing to a bed to be found on set. Reporters had a field day with this story, and it later became "fact" that Lugosi eschewed the traditional comforts of a bed at home and rather slept inside a custom built casket, which was untrue.

- *Bela was hypnotized for the 1940 film* **Black Friday.** At the climax of *Black Friday*, Lugosi's claustrophobic character gets locked in a box and dies a screaming, horrible death, scratching the walls and pleading for help. The studio circulated rumors that Bela had been hypnotized in order to make his death scene more realistic. This was basically a publicity stunt, as Bela was afraid that if he were to be hypnotized, his wife would lead the hypnotist into making post-hypnotic suggestions that would alter his behavior, such as giving up wine or cigars! In actuality, Lugosi played his death scene so believably that audiences were none the wiser.

- *Bela refused to lose his Hungarian accent.* This is true, actually. Universal set him up with a diction coach so that he would be able to soften his accent, thereby making him "easier to understand" for American audiences. Lugosi attended two lessons and refused to take any more, claiming that his accent was what got him the role of Dracula and that's what the audiences wanted to hear. He may have been correct, but this also may have contributed to his typecasting as the "evil-foreign-mad doctor" type that plagued him later on.

The first of the Lugosi/Wood collaborations was entitled I Led Two Lives, a semi-autobiographical film about a transvestite named Glen (Ed Wood) who dressed in angora and became the feminine "Glenda". Lugosi was later shocked to learn the film's true subject matter, as he was only given the part of the script that contained his monologue. But he was paid $1,000 for one day's worth of work, money that was sorely needed. The film was later titled *Glen or Glenda, or How I Changed My Sex*.

Lugosi next starred in Wood's *Bride of the Atom* (later to be called *Bride of the Monster*) which paid a little more than what he made in *Glen or Glenda*, but at the cost of a breakneck schedule that took a toll on Bela's health.

Now immune to the effects of any prescription narcotics, his doctor ordered him to detox so that they could begin anew with non-habit forming medications. Lugosi was a charter member of the Screen Actor's Guild, and so he contacted them in order to use the Guild-owned rehabilitation facilities offered in Sherman Oaks for retired screen actors. But to his horror, he was denied entry because he hadn't made a Union film in five years. Bela argued that he had just made *Bride of the Atom*, a union film, but since it had yet to see release, it didn't count in the eyes of the SAG. It was truly outrageous that the union that he helped create and gave so much money and support to over the years, precisely in case of an emergency like this, turned his back on him when he needed it the most. Lugosi later lit a cigar with his SAG card and called the Guild "monsters."

Having no money to cover his hospital stay, Bela had to pitifully go before the Los Angeles County Psychopathic Court to plead his case for voluntary commitment. In those days, a judge had to decide if you were in a position to one day pay back your hospital expenses after you were released, in order to admit you into the facilities on good faith. Judge Wallace Ware took great pity on Bela's story (slightly embellished) and allowed him entrance into the Psyche Ward.

"Pull de stringk!" Lugosi, as the omnipotent narrator of Glen or Glenda, *gave it his all even though the films of Ed Wood were some of the worst ever made.*

Headlines soon broke out all over the country: BELA LUGOSI ADMITTED FOR NARCOTIC ADDICTION; LUGOSI- HEROIN JUNKIE; BELA LUGOSI CLAIMS ADDICTION TO MORPHINE FOR 20 YEARS.

The press surrounded his bedside for the next few days. Bela gave more interviews from his hospital bed in three days than he had given in the last twenty years put together. Fan mail began pouring in, the likes of which he hadn't seen in years. *The Bride of the Monster* was finally released, the proceeds from the premiere going to cover Lugosi's hospital bills. Even Frank Sinatra stopped in to visit, and left Lugosi a "substantial" sum of cash, according to Kitty Kelly. After Sinatra left, Lugosi was reduced to tears by the act of kindness. He had never before met Frank Sinatra and yet the famous star was moved enough by Lugosi's plight that he wanted to help in any way he could. "This," Lugosi said, "was the way it was when actors took care of their own. Damn the union."

One of the fan letters he received during his stay peaked his interest above all others. It was from a young fan named Hope Lininger, who wished him well and signed her letter "a dash of Hope." The two built up a correspondence that later led to marriage in 1955.

Soon after being released from rehab, Bela was chosen to appear in his last major film, 1956's *The*

"Dracula" is Dope Addict

Typical 1955 tabloid fodder following Lugosi's admittance into rehab. *"Dracula is a Dope Addict"* was actually one of the less-sensational headlines to emerge from the incident.

Lugosi's first cigar after entering rehab. As part of his detox regimen, he was not allowed to smoke at all for nearly a month. He made due on a steady diet of Polish Snuff and cigar-scrap chewing tobacco.

With Lon Chaney Jr. In 1956's *The Black Sleep*, Lugosi's final official film.

Plan 9 From Outer Space: Supposedly the "worst film ever made." Lugosi is joined here by Finnish model turned horror host Vampira (Maila Nurmi) and Swedish wrestler turned actor Tor Johnson (also a noted Snuser).

Black Sleep. Though it was produced by a second-tier studio, it was distributed as an "A" picture by United Artists, who sent the stars Basil Rathbone, Bela Lugosi, Lon Cheney Jr, John Carradine, Tor Johnson and Akim Tamiroff on a publicity tour that Lugosi greatly enjoyed. Of all the other stars in the film, Lugosi spoke the most at these press junkets, partly due to ego and partly because his role in the film of Casimir the Mute required no dialogue.

Meanwhile, Ed Wood came around again with another "idea" treatment, this one for a project entitled *The Vampire's Tomb*. With just a title to work on, Wood filmed about three minutes of Lugosi stalking around a "graveyard" (actually Tor Johnson's front yard) to show to prospective backers. He also shot some bizarre, hallucinatory footage of Lugosi as a sci-fi Dracula type for another idea of Wood's called *Ghouls on the Moon*.

None of these projects came to pass, however. On August 16, 1956, Lugosi died of a heart attack while lying on his couch. For the previous two days, he had been speaking incoherently, leading some to suspect that he may have had a stroke that triggered the heart attack. The 73 year old actor left behind a young widow and a 16 year old son. He was buried at Holy Cross Cemetery in Los Angeles, in full Dracula regalia. Hundreds came to mourn his passing, and a renewed interest in the horror films of the 30's and 40's brought young children under Lugosi's spell just mere months after he died. The 1958 launch of *Famous Monsters of Filmland* magazine was instrumental in keeping the Lugosi legacy alive, and in its 55 year history, almost every issue featured articles, blurbs or stills about Bela.

In 1959, Ed Wood released Lugosi's "final film," *Plan 9 From Outer Space*, which has taken the #1 spot on many a critic's list as The Worst Movie Ever Made. The three minutes of footage shot for *The Vampires Tomb* of Lugosi walking around Tor Johnson's yard was incorporated into an inane plot about space aliens, zombies, and flying saucers. The remainder of Lugosi's scenes were played by Wood's chiropractor Tom Mason. Mason, at 6'4" and 160 pounds was a poor replacement for the 180 pound, 6'1" Lugosi. To make matters worse, the actor looked absolutely nothing like Lugosi, and so his face was covered by his cape throughout the rest of the picture. If you have somehow gone your life without seeing this "film", do yourself a favor and watch it. It's a totally unforgettable experience.

During the 1970's, the original *Dracula* was re-released theatrically to a new generation of fans. This renewed interest in Lugosi's films prompted his son to file suit against Universal Pictures, who were still profiting from his father's image. Initially, the Lugosi family won and Universal was ordered to pay millions of dollars in due royalties. However, Universal won under appeal and until 1986's *Celebrities Rights Act*, the estate of a dead entertainer had no control over how their likeness was used.

1979 also brought proto-goth band Bauhaus's single *Bela Lugosi's Dead*, widely considered the very first goth song ever recorded. The song was basically a tribute poem written by the band's bassist David J., as an acknowledgement to the man who he felt was responsible for the entire "vampire movement" that was starting to give way in the punk scene. The refrain summed up Lugosi's legacy in three succinct lines:

The Count...
Bela Lugosi's Dead.
Undead, Undead, Undead!

After *Plan 9's* 1959 release, Ed Wood boasted (or threatened, depending on how you looked at it) that he still contained the test footage for *Ghouls on the Moon* featuring the final footage of Lugosi ever shot. Described by Hollywood Babylon author Kenneth Anger as "wild stuff", Wood tried to find backing for the film almost until his death in the late 70's. Unfortunately, when the film reel was unearthed almost twenty years after it was shot, the quality had degraded so badly that it was considered unsalvageable, and so *Ghouls on the Moon* remains Lugosi's final, lost film.

Lugosi's career took another peak in the 1990's when filmmaker Tim Burton helmed the movie *Ed Wood*, which was based on Wood's "golden years" in Hollywood and his friendship with the aging Lugosi. Both Johnny Depp as Ed Wood and Martin Landau as Lugosi were nominated for best actors, with Landau (very deservingly) taking home the Oscar for Best Supporting Actor.

While a good film on its own, the story could hardly be called factually accurate in any way. The plot took a number of liberties with established fact, and painted Lugosi in a very unflattering light in some aspects. Many who knew both Wood and Lugosi in real life were tempted to sue the studio for defamation, but nothing ever came of it.

Today, with the modern vampire craze in full swing (fueled by the phenomenally successful *Twilight* and *True Blood* series, among many others) it would seem that Lugosi is poised to make a comeback any time now. If there's one thing we've learned about the vampire/horror revivals of years past is that the younger audiences come back to the source.

One day, your teenaged daughter will walk in with a copy of the latest teen-vamp-romance-soft-porn-for-middle-schoolers best seller about "sparkly" bloodsuckers. But don't be discouraged, as she may come back home the next week with a DVD copy of Hammer's *Horror of Dracula*, the silent version of *Nosferatu*, or dare we suggest-the remastered Blu-Ray of Lugosi's 1931 *Dracula*? One could only hope that the future Children of the Night will appreciate the founder of their faith.

Bela, as he appeared in his funeral casket.

The simple, unpretentious headstone that marks his grave at the Holy Cross Cemetery. Thousands of fans from all over the world have flocked to his gravesite to pay their last respects.

Martin Landau, in his Academy Award winning role as Lugosi in the 1994 Tim Burton Biopic *Ed Wood*.

BELA LUGOSI ON STAGE

The following screenography is in no way complete; there were hundreds of minor appearances and one-off shows that Lugosi took part in. Only listed are the major productions and revivals that he was known to star in.

- Brigadier General Ocksay **(1902)**
- We're Married
- Claire Felho

- Stubborn King David **(1903)**
- Maria Stuart
- The Arabian Nights
- Monna Vanna
- The Bat
- Fedora
- Trilby

- Husband in Reserve **(1904)**
- Himfy's Song
- The Golden Rooster
- In the Sign of the Cross
- Rank and Style
- The Admirable Crichton
- The Iron Maker
- The Mustache

- Romeo & Juliet **(1910)**
- The Parasites
- Golden Man
- Operetta
- Lady of the Camellias
- The Dolova Nabob's Daughter
- The Devil
- Typhoon
- Fetters
- The Mailboy and his Sister
- What Every Woman Knows
- The Iron Maker
- Honor of the Sword
- The Cowboy
- The Martyrs of Szigetvari
- The Government Commissioner
- Bank Ban

- The Eaglet
- The Balkan Princess
- The Foolish Virgin
- The Woman Child

- Baccarat **(1911)**
- Orange Blossom
- I Tired of Margaret
- The Sacred Grove
- Yellow Lilly
- The Medico
- Lotti's Colonels
- Othello
- The Scoundrels
- The Golden Wedding
- Doctor Robin
- The Thief
- The Merry Widow
- Hamlet
- The Taming of the Shrew
- The Witch
- Viola: Outlaw of the Lowlands
- The Ignominious
- Fata Morgana
- The Emmigrant
- Puppet Show
- Silent Bells
- Scandal
- The Yellow Colt
- Trilby
- The Teacher
- Secretary of State
- The Genius
- The Rape of the Sabine Women
- Anatol
- Anna Karenina
- Yellow Lily
- The Call of Life

- The Geisha **(1912)**

- Anna Karenina
- Yellow Lilly

- The Iron Maker **(1913)**
- The Tragedy of Man
- Mary Ann
- Cyrano de Bergerac
- Maria Stuart
- Richard III
- Caesar and Cleopatra
- Golden Man
- King John
- A Midsummer's Night Dream
- Tartuffe
- The Captivity of Rakoczi II
- The Witch
- Hamlet
- The Torches
- Byzantium
- The Oath of Eva Draghy
- The Adopted Father
- Hernani
- The Confidant
- Faust
- Endre and Johanna
- Lady of the Camellias
- Visla
- Dance of the Fools
- King Lear
- The Last Day
- The Attaché
- Convention Commissar
- Count Essex
- Marie Antoinette
- The One-Time Prince
- Monna Vanna
- Christmas Dream

- Eva, the Witch **(1914)**
- The Matyo Wedding
- Macbeth
- The Borrowed Castle
- Aesop
- The Woman's Friend
- The Umbrella is up

- Liliomfi
- The Principal
- The Story of a Career
- The Iron Maker
- King John
- Julius Caesar
- Contenders for the Throne
- The Notary Public of Peleske

- Maria Stuart **(1916)**
- The Passion
- Hamlet
- Macbeth
- Othello
- Romeo and Juliet
- The Deserter
- Hamlet
- Henry IV
- Aesop
- Susie
- Don Carlos
- The Story of a Poor Kid
- The Three Bodyguards
- The Taming of the Shrew
- Festive Play

- Keleman, the Mason **(1917)**
- The Tragedy of Man
- The P.O.W.
- The Dissenters
- King John
- A Midsummer Night's Dream
- Mary Magdalene
- Grandmother

- As You Like It **(1918)**
- Madam Charlotte
- Lone King Laszlo
- Emperor Joseph II
- Lady of the Camellias
- Greek Fire
- Romeo and Juliet
- Byzantium

Lugosi relaxing in his Hollywood den.

1: Pipe, most likely a Dunhill.   **2:** Glass Ashtray built into the chair's armrest.   **3:** Mounted oil lamp. Lugosi preferred to read by lamplight rather than electrical light.   **4:** Wooden snuffbox (left) and box of cigars (right), the latter being a gift from Boris Karloff. Lugosi seems to be using them here as paperweights. **5:** "Trick" ottoman. The lid opened to reveal a massive humidor stocked full of cigars. Purchased while vacationing in Egypt.   **6:** Pipe rest with matchbox holder and ashtray, next to a pot of dying flowers. **7:** Small piperack with tiny glass humidor.   **8:** Metal humidor canister.

- Richard III
- Henry VIII
- Bagatelle

- The Kingdom of Sancho Panza **(1919)**

- The Tragedy of Man **(1922)**
- The Red Poppy [*first English speaking role*]

- The Werewolf **(1924)**

- Arabesque **(1925)**
- Open House

- The Devil in the Cheese **(1926)**

- Dracula **(1927)**

- Murdered Alive **(1932)**

- Murder at the Vanities **(1933)**

- Tovarich (1937)

- Dracula (1943)
- Arsenic and Old Lace

- No Traveler Returns (1945)

- The Devil Also Dreams (1950)

- Dracula (1951-1952)

- Devil's Paradise (1956) (*Final stage appearance*)

Even though he had played the role hundreds of times, Lugosi never failed to give an outstanding performance in any of the Dracula revivals that he appeared in over the course of 25 years.

STE

Bela Lugosi: Complete Filmography

The Hungarian Films (In all of Lugosi's Hungarian films, he was billed variously as either Arisztid Olt, Olt Arisztad, or Bela Blasko)

- The Colonel (1917)[1]
- Leoni Leo[1]
- A Régiséggyutjö[1]
- The Wedding Song[1]
- A Leopard (1918)[2]
- Casanova[2]
- Spring Tempest[1]
- Masked Ball[1]
- Lulu[1]
- Struggle for Life[1]
- Lili[2]
- The Picture of Dorian Gray[1] (AKA *The Royal Life*)
- 99[1]

The German Films

- Necklace of the Dead (1919)[1]
- The Curse of Man (1920)[3]
- The Curse of Man: Daughter of Labor[3]
- The Curse of Man: Ecstasy of Billions[3]
- Daughter of Night[3]
- Dance on the Volcano Part One: Sybil Young[1]
- Dance on the Volcano Part Two: Death of the Grand Duke[1]
- The Woman In The Dolphin[1]
- The Devil Worshippers[1]
- Slave of a Foreign Power (aka *Hypnosis*)[1]
- Slaveowner from Kansas City[1]
- Nat Pinkerton In the Fight[1]
- Der Januskopf (AKA *The Head of Janus*; *Dr. Jekyll and Mr. Hyde*)[1]
- Leatherstocking (AKA *Deerslayer; Deerslayer and Chingachgook*)¶
- The Body is Burning[1]
- On the Brink of Paradise[1]
- The Last of the Mohicans (AKA *Deerslayer Part Two; Leatherstocking: Part Two*)[1]
- Caravan of Death (AKA *On the Brink of Paradise Part Two*)[1]
- Johann Hopkins the 3rd (1921)[1]
- Her Highness, The Dancer (AKA *The Ordeal of Eva Grunwald*) (1922)[1]Φ

The Early American Films

- The Silent Command (1923)
- The Rejected Woman (1924)
- He Who Gets Slapped Ω

---

[1] *Considered a "lost" film, no known complete copies exist.*

[2] *"Lost" film, but some footage is known to exist.*

[3] *"The Curse of Man" was an ongoing series of films. Lugosi had a bit role in the first film and a different, more prominent role in the second and third films. The second and third films were edited together in a condensed version released in the US as "Daughter of Night". Considered lost for seven decades, a copy of "Daughter of Night" was found in 1990 and is the only remaining version of any of the films known to exist.*

¶ *"Leatherstocking" and "Last of the Mohicans" were two back-to-back features adapted from James Fenimore Cooper's novels. The American cut of the first film (entitled "Deerslayer") was discovered about ten years ago and is heavily edited from the original German cut.*

Φ *This film was banned by the German censors upon release and all copies were ordered to be destroyed. A heavily edited version entitled "The Ordeal of Eva Grunwald" was approved and released and is now considered lost.*

Ω *MGM Studio's very first movie. The only surviving print runs 75 minutes (down from the original 90 minutes) and Bela Lugosi's scenes may be missing from this condensed version. It's hard to confirm either way as Lugosi's role was a bit part performed completely in clown makeup. Some Lugosi historians question whether he was even IN the film at all as the details remains scarce.*

- The Midnight Girl (1925)
- Daughters Who Pay
- Punchinello (1926)[1]
- The Last Performance (AKA *The Last Call*) (1927)*
- How To Handle Women (AKA *Fresh Every Hour; The Prince of Knuts*) (1928)
- The Veiled Woman[1] (1929)
- Prisoners [1][2]
- The Thirteenth Chair (AKA *The 13th Chair*)[3]
- Such Men are Dangerous (1930) ¶
- Viennese Nights Φ
- King of Jazz ±
- Wild Company
- Renegades
- Oh, For A Man!
- Dracula (1931)
- Drácula Θ
- Women of all Nations (cameo)
- Broadminded
- 50 Million Frenchmen (cameo)
- The Black Camel (AKA *Charlie Chan in The Black Camel*)

Post-Dracula Success; Peak of Stardom

- Murders in the Rue Morgue (1932)
- Chandu the Magician (AKA *Chandu*)
- White Zombie
- The Death Kiss ∞
- Island of Lost Souls
- The Whispering Shadow (1933) ε
- Hollywood on Parade Part 8 (Short subject)
- Night of Terror (AKA *He Lived to Kill*)
- International House
- The Devil's In Love (cameo)
- The Black Cat (1934)
- The Gift of Gab (cameo)
- The Return of Chandu (Serial)¥
- The Return of Chandu (Feature)¥
- Chandu on the Magic Island ¥

* *Technically, Lugosi's first sound film, although* Performance *was an early "Hybrid" Silent/talkie film, meaning that two versions were produced: one for silent theaters and one for the early sound projectors with a soundtrack dubbed in postproduction. In addition to playing a bit part in the American version of the film, Lugosi dubbed star Conrad Veidt's lines for the Hungarian version. Also Lugosi's first film for Universal.*

[1] *Considered a "lost" film, no known complete copies exist.*

[2] *Hybrid silent/talkie film.*

[3] *Another Hybrid soundie. This marked the first time that American audiences got to hear Lugosi's voice in a film. Silent version is lost, but the sound version is known to exist in private collections.*

¶ *Lugosi's first "sound-only" film. From here out, all of his subsequent films were "talkies."*

Φ *Lugosi's first color film (Technicolor).*

± *Lugosi's second color film (Technicolor). Lugosi did not appear in the American version (which still exists), but he hosted the Hungarian edition (now lost). At least nine different foreign versions were released which featured native stars introducing the segments in their own language. This film is also something of a curio for fans of the rock group Nirvana as it features actor Delbert Cobain, great-uncle of Kurt Cobain.*

Θ *This Spanish-language version of "Dracula" was shot simultaneously (at night) on the same sets as the American version and starred a Spanish and Mexican cast. Though the title role was played by Carlos Villiaris, some of Lugosi's long shots and from-behind footage from the American film made it into the Spanish version of* Dracula.

∞ *Mostly Black & White, but featured some hand-tinted color sequences.*

ε *Twelve part serial, later condensed into a feature version under the same title.*

¥ *"The Return of Chandu" was a twelve part serial, later condensed into two 65 minute features entitled* Return of Chandu *and* Chandu on the Magic Island.

- The Mysterious Mr. Wong (1935)
- The Best Man Wins
- Mark of the Vampire **(publicity shot at left)**
- The Raven
- Phantom Ship (AKA *Mystery of the Mary Celeste*)
- Murder By Television
- The Invisible Ray (1936)
- Revolt of the Zombies[1]
- Postal Inspector
- Shadow of Chinatown[2]
- SOS Coastguard (1937) ∩

"Horror/ Monster Movie Period"; Gradual Descent into Typecast Mediocrity & Low Budget "B" Pictures

- Son of Frankenstein (1939)
- The Gorilla
- The Phantom Creeps ∩
- Ninotchka
- The Dark Eyes of London (AKA *Human Monster*)
- The Saint's Double Trouble (1940)
- Black Friday
- Bela Lugosi: Hypnotized (Short Subject)
- The Devil Bat
- Fantasia*
- You'll Find Out (AKA *Here Come the Boogie Men*)
- The Invisible Ghost (1941)
- The Black Cat
- Spooks Run Wild
- The Wolf Man
- The Black Dragons (1942)
- The Ghost of Frankenstein
- Night Monster (AKA *House of Mystery*)
- The Corpse Vanishes
- Bowery at Midnight
- Frankenstein Meets the Wolf Man (1943)
- The Ape Man (AKA *Lock Your Doors; The Gorilla Strikes; They Creep in the Night*)
- Ghosts on the Loose (AKA *Ghosts in the Night*)
- Return of the Vampire (1944)
- Voodoo Man (AKA *Tiger Man*)
- One Body Too Many
- Return of the Ape Man
- Zombies on Broadway (1945)
- The Bodysnatcher
- Genius at Work (1946)
- Scared to Death (1947) ≈
- Abbott and Costello Meet Frankenstein (1948)
- Seeing Stars (Short subject) (1951)
- Lock up Your Daughters ⌂
- Vampire over London (1952) (AKA *My Son the Vampire; Old Mother Riley Meets the Vampire; Dracula's Desire*)
- Bela Lugosi Meets a Brooklyn Gorilla (AKA *The Boys From Brooklyn*)
- Glen or Glenda (1953) (AKA *I Changed My Sex; I Led Two Lives*)
- Bride of the Monster (1955) (AKA *Bride of the Atom*)
- The Black Sleep (1956)
- Plan 9 From Outer Space (1959) (*AKA Grave Robbers From Outer Space*)**

[1] *"Revolt of the Zombies" features archival footage of Lugosi taken from "White Zombie."*

[2] *Fifteen part serial, later released in a condensed feature version under the same title.*

∩ *Twelve part serial, later released in a condensed feature version under the same title.*

* *Though he didn't appear in* Fantasia *per se, Lugosi filmed live action footage of the character Chernabog which was used as a reference for the animators.*

≈ *Lugosi's third and final color film (not counting* Fantasia *and* Death Kiss*). The only other color footage that exists of Lugosi is from the 1943* Screen Snapshots *newsreel about the war effort in which he can be seen donating blood.*

⌂ *Feature length British docu-comedy made up entirely of footage from previous Lugosi films. Rarely screened and now considered lost.*

** *Released three years after his death,* Plan 9 *featured stock footage of Lugosi walking around his front yard (and in a cemetery) that was shot by director Ed Wood shortly before Bela's passing. Widely considered "the worst movie ever made."*

STE

BELA AND THE BROWN LEAF

A RETROSPECTIVE LOOK AT LUGOSI'S TOBACCO HABITS

Bela Lugosi's first experiment with tobacco was from stealing snuff from his father's snuffbox at the age of 5. His father owned a bank, and he would keep a complimentary tin of snuff on his desk for the customers to pinch from. Lugosi learned to snuff by watching the Rumanians and Gypsies that would come in and try to borrow money from his father.

"The Gypsies used snuff in a way unlike the other travelers that passed through. They would put it in their nose, in their ears. They would rub it over their teeth and gums. Some would wipe it under their eyes. The Gypsy truly was unique in that regard."

He would smoke his first cigar at age 7. "I wanted to imitate my father one day by rolling my own cigar out of leaves, probably tea leaves. It tasted awful!"

He recalled his father's evening pipe ritual. "After returning from work, my mother would have my father's pipe cleaned and filled with his favorite tobacco. That is what Hungarian wives are trained to do. They warm their husband's cigars and light them correctly so that the leaf doesn't burn unevenly. They make sure the pipe is always clean and sweetened with honey. I once saw my father knock my mother across the room because she forgot to let the pipe dry after cleaning it, making the tobacco wet and unsmokable. He was quite the

> Quite simply, my dear, tobacco is the greatest pleasure that we have ever discovered. It does not matter if it is chewed, smoked, sniffed or anything else... It was put here by The Almighty to sooth our jagged edges. I know of no other miracle like it in nature.
>
> -1939 interview

cruel man at times."

As a young man, Bela attempted to smoke pipes in the same fashion, but he was notorious for never cleaning them and allowing the cake to build up so thick that it was virtually impossible to pack it with tobacco. This was a chore that he considered to be a woman's work. Therefore, until he married his fourth wife, Lillian, he mainly smoked cigars.

"During the war [WW1], cigars were very scarce for the Hungarian army. But we had plenty of cigarettes, which we confiscated from the Germans. Therefore I developed a habit to cigarette smoking that I have always somewhat regretted." In one interview, he said that he quit smoking cigarettes after the war once he was able to get cigars again. In another interview, he claimed to have given them up because cigarette smoking was always regarded as a feminine habit in Hungary, and he never felt quite right smoking them.

And in yet another interview, the reason that he said he gave cigarettes up for good was because while his son, Bela Jr. was being born, he walked around the hospital in circles, chainsmoking in order to calm his nerves. "A

Doctor shouts to me, 'Hey Bela, do you not know that those cigarettes are what is causing you to be 'so nervous?' The nicotine, you know. You do not get nicotine from cigars and pipes like you do cigarettes, and I stopped then."

Lugosi began a love affair with fine cigars from then on, buying brands made from all over the world and keeping them in massive humidors. While on a vacation to Egypt with his wife, he spotted a unique ottoman that actually housed a humidor inside that cold hold up to 400 cigars. He had it shipped back to the states for his "smoking den" and even went out to purchase a matching chair for it.

By 1941, his cigar habit was in full force. When doing a live performance on stage, his wife Lillian would wait in the wings, slowly puffing on one of Bela's large Havanas so that he could sneak back-

Rare 1938 portrait of Bela with a cigarette. He preferred Fatima cigarettes, as did Jack Webb at one point.

Lugosi with a seated Ed Wood, a couple of years before Bela's death.

stage between acts and take a couple of puffs before his scenes.

With a "traditional" Hungarian wife now in hand, Bela finally found someone to clean his pipes for him. Lillian would lovingly fill each pipe with rubbing alcohol to let the cake and dottle soften and would place it upright on the rack so that the alcohol wouldn't spill out. The next day she would take a pipecleaner to it and give it one more scrub with Scotch before rubbing honey inside the bowl to give it the sweetness that Bela was fond of. This was quite a task, considering that Bela always kept about 40 pipes on-hand at any given time!

Lyle Talbot recalls meeting Lugosi on set one day and stood talking with him while Bela packed his pipe. He noticed that Bela was barely able to fit any tobacco into the bowl. "The cake inside the bowl was a half inch thick! I took my pocket knife out and cut it down and told him to go buy a reamer." Even though Lugosi kept a clean pipe, he didn't know that you had to periodically ream the cake down to keep a clean bowl.

But Bela's fortunes weren't always so great, and so when he couldn't afford his clear Havanas, he would resort to the drugstore favorites. Recalled one of his acquaintances, Bela alternated between El Producto cigars (which Bela jokingly called "El Ropo El Stinkos") and the Italian Toscani line (De Nobili, Padroni, Petri) which he enjoyed greatly, even though he derisively called them his "Guinea Stinkers."

Bela's attitude about female smokers was very much old-fashioned. Even though he had wife Lillian puff away on his cigars while he was busy on stage, he thought that lady smokers were trying to be "too mannish" and that they should stick to snuff. If they absolutely needed to smoke, then it should be a cigarette, and never a pipe or cigar.

His wife Lillian recalled one night that on the way to a party, she decided to rile Bela up in retaliation for an argument they had earlier. Coming up to a gas station, she told the driver to stop. "What are we stopping for?" asked Bela.

SMOKING AS A SCIENCE: *Smoking is a science as Bela Lugosi, motion picture actor takes it. He has a collection of 32 pipes, all of different sizes. The size of the meal determines the size of the pipe he selects for an evening. Besides the pipe in his mouth, there are 12 on the table. [Life Magazine, 23 Jan., 1935]*

Note the infamous humidor ottoman that was probably stacked full of premium cigars.

"I've decided to start smoking," Lillian answered.

Bela was visibly annoyed. "Well what brand shall I get you, then?" Having never smoked before, Lillian was at a loss for words. "Bah!" he said, jumping out of the car and returning with a pack. He tossed it on her lap and told the driver to continue.

"I think I took two drags and tossed the rest of them away," Lillian recalled laughingly.

Carol Borland, his young co-star in 1935's *Mark of the Vampire*, recalled a similar incident. "I was sitting with a group of girls at a café, and they were passing around cigarettes. I didn't smoke, but I wanted to fit in, so I took one and lit it. I felt the entire time that I was doing something wrong, and I turned around and through the glass there was Bela, glaring at me disapprovingly! I never touched another cigarette again."

During the last ten years of his life, Bela had a daily ritual. He would walk down Hollywood Boulevard and stop in at his favorite tobacco shop. Each day he would buy a new premium cigar, one that he had never tried before, along with his usual pack of "Guinea Stinkers". The tobacconist once asked him what he planned to do when he had finally sampled his last new cigar, to which Bela replied "I'll probably keel over and die!" About a week before his death, Bela told the shopkeep to find some new cigar brands. "I'm on my last one!"

The stop at the tobacco store was just part of the long walk Lugosi took each day to stay in shape. He could be seen pretty much every day, dressed in Bermuda shorts and a short-sleeved button up shirt. (Bela had taken to dressing as comfortably as possible in his older age.) After the tobacco store, he would usually duck into a nearby shoestore, which had a comfortable bench that he could nod away in, De Nobili in his mouth.

Once a week, Bela would stop in to a barber shop on his route. Said the barber, "Mine was a unique shop for the fifties. I didn't allow smoking inside, because I just didn't like the smell of smoke."

This greatly angered Bela Lugosi, who felt that it was his God-given right to smoke anywhere he wanted. So friends recall that each time before he went to the barber, Bela would pick up a bag of Mail Pouch chewing tobacco to take with him to this particular barber.

"It was always the same thing," said his friend. "Bela would climb into the chair, lean over, and spit a giant wad of tobacco juice on the floor. The barber would always say 'Why'd you do that, Bela?' And Bela would reply 'Vat, did you expect me to swallow it? Buy a spittoon or let me smoke my cigar!'" The barber did neither, so Bela would come in once a week, get a shave and a haircut, and leave a puddle of tobacco juice on the floor.

When Bela admitted himself to the rehabilitation hospital to kick his addiction to opiates, he had no idea that they were going to put him on a strict 20 day regimen of not smoking. Ed Wood recalls:

"Bela grabs my by the sleeve and says 'Eddie, they say no cigars for twenty days. *Twenty days!*' So we concoct this scheme where I bring him chewing tobacco, but the nurses caught it because he had to keep spitting into a cup. So our last resort was some Polish snuff, which kept him occupied for the next couple of weeks."

1992 US Postage Stamp Honoring Bela Lugosi, himself a lifelong stamp collector.

When Bela Lugosi died on August 16th, 1956, he had an open pack of Parodi cigars next to him on the couch. This pack was buried with him, along with his Dracula cloak and ring. His family said that he would have wanted it that way.

There is a strange postscript to this tale, though. When Bela was being escorted by horse and carriage to his final resting place in Holy Cross Cemetery, the procession went down "Bela's route" along Hollywood Boulevard. When the hearse reached the tobacco store that Lugosi stopped in every day, the horses stopped dead in their tracks. Nothing could get them to move from the spot in front of the tobacco store.

Finally, the driver leaned into the back and whispered into the casket. "C'mon, Bela. You're holding everyone up." The horses immediately resumed their stride towards the cemetery.

Was it Bela's spirit, hoping to stop in one last time to his favorite store to sample a cigar that he may have missed? Who knows. People have even claimed to see Lugosi's ghost frequenting the boulevard, cigar in hand, for over 50 years. Let's hope he finally finds that perfect blend that will let him forever rest in peace.

STE

Presented for posterity with the utmost respect for Lugosi and his family, and not for ghoulish exploitation purposes, is the final photo of Bela, taken as he appeared in his casket, August 18th, 1956.

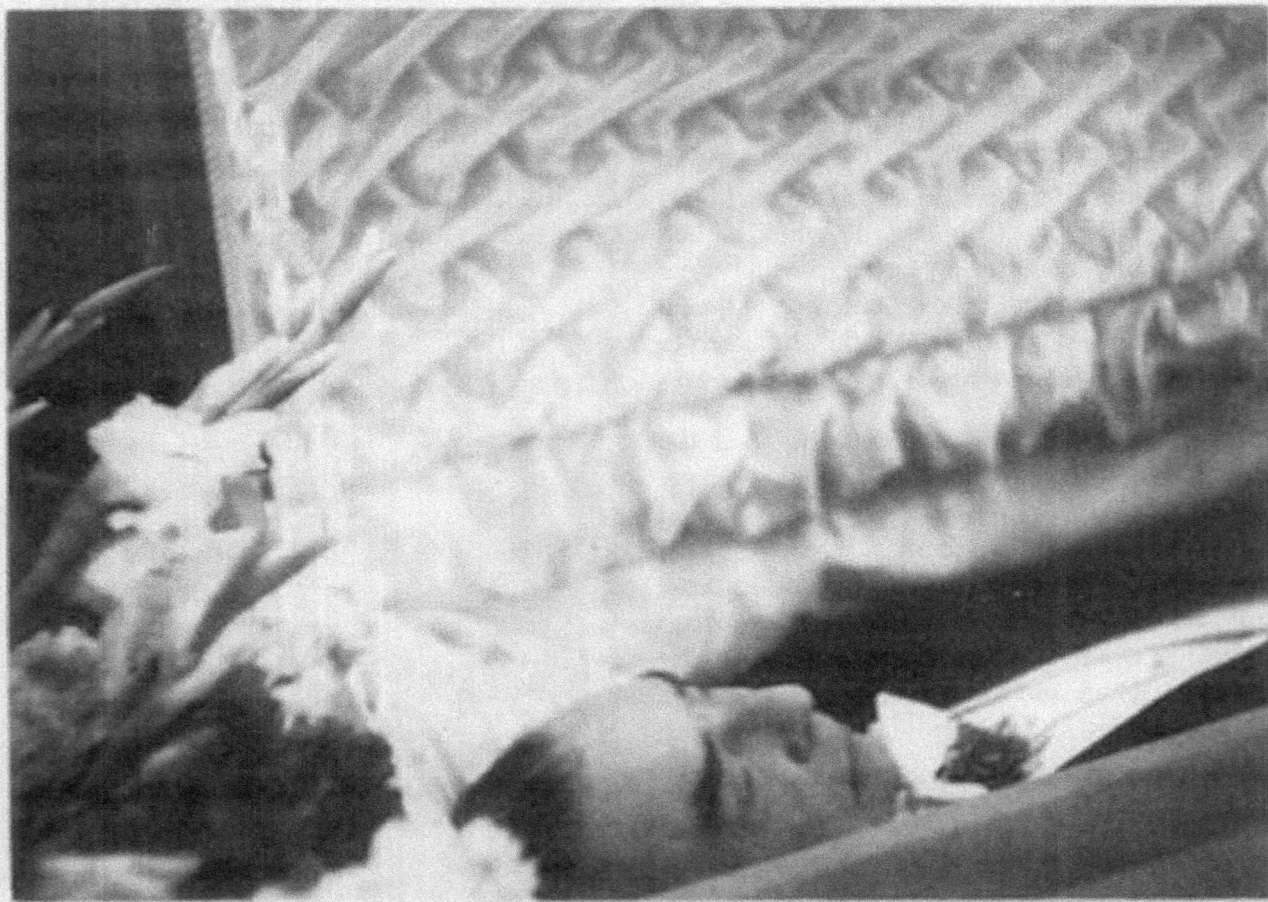

LUGOSI IN HIS OWN WORDS

Presenting here a fairly rare studio press questionnaire from 1935, filled out by Bela as he was shooting the film Murder by Television. *Enjoy!*

CAMEO PICTURES CORPORATION   PART OF:
BIOGRAPHICAL INFORMATION   IN:

This is to insure accuracy in our publicity, and to provide complete and accurate material necessary for newspaper and magazine stories.

1. Screen name *Bela Lugosi* Real name in full *was Bela Blasko - legally changed to - Bela Lugosi*

2. Height *6' 1"* Nickname *None*

3. Nationality *Hungarian* Color of hair *Brown*

   Weight *170 lbs.* Color of eyes *Blue*

4. Birthplace *Lugos, Hungary* Date *October 20, 1888*

5. Education _____ Highschool _____ College *✓*

6. Parents names *(Father) Stephen Blasko - Paula (Mother) von Vojnics* Both living? *no*

   Where *Buried at Lugos, Hungary* Father's business *was - Bank President*

   Famous ancestors or relatives *None*

   Brothers or sisters names *Vilma - Lajos - Laszlo*

   Earliest childhood ambition *Highway Bandit*

7. Present ambition *Dude Ranch*

8. First occupation *Actor* Where? *Travelling Repertoire*

   Past and present business interests apart from the screen *None*

   _____

9. How did your career begin? (Amateur shows, college dramatics, beauty contests, started by famous actor or director, for a lark)

   College Dramatics

10. Stage debut in *Romeo* Year *1906* Place *Lugosi Hungary*

    Broadway debut *Red Poppy* Year *1923* Starred with Estelle Co

    Last play *Murder-in-the-Vanities* Year *1933* Place *New York City - Wynnwood*

    Other important plays *In America - "Dracula"*

    In Hungary - All the great parts in literature

    Stock in what cities *None*

11. Film debut in *"The Silent Command"* Year *1923* Star *Heavy - with an all star cast*

    First large part in *Same* Year *-* Star *-*

    First talkie *"Prisoners"* Year *1929* Star *Corinne Griffith*

    Last picture *Mark of the Vampires* Year *1935* Star *All Star at - M.G.M.*

    Other pictures (Next to last, etc.) *"Mysterious Mr. Wong"*

    "Return of Chandu" - "Black Cat" -

-2-

12. Favorite Screen role "Count Dracula" in "Dracula"
13. Favorite Stage role Cyrano de Bergerac in Cyrano de Bergerac
14. Prefer screen to stage? yes why Variety
15. What type of role have you played most? great characters
16. What type do you prefer Human interest
17. Favorite stage players None
18. Favorite screen players None Mickey Mouse
19. Favorite playrights ———
20. Favorite books Social Science and Economy

21. Favorite authors none -
22. Favorite sports to watch Soccer
23. Favorite sports to play Golf
24. HIGHSPOTS of your life (in chronological order)

    1 to 10 years ⎫ it is
    10 to 20 years ⎬ No ones business
    20 to 30 years ⎭

    Ad infinitum

25. CLOTHES prefer conservative or modish
              ready made or tailored conservative tailored

    Favor sports or formal wear? sports

    Favorite colors bright

    Favorite materials flannels

26. Have you any beauty secrets such as methods of make-up, care of
    hair, eyes, hands, skin, facials, massages, oils, creams?

    None

27. How do you keep in condition? (Health institute, daily or weekly
    massages, sun-baths, setting-up exercises, sports?) golf

28. FOOD favorite dish Stuffed Cabbage Like to cook? ———
    Between meal snacks No Bedtime snack? No
    Favorite recipe: Dish:

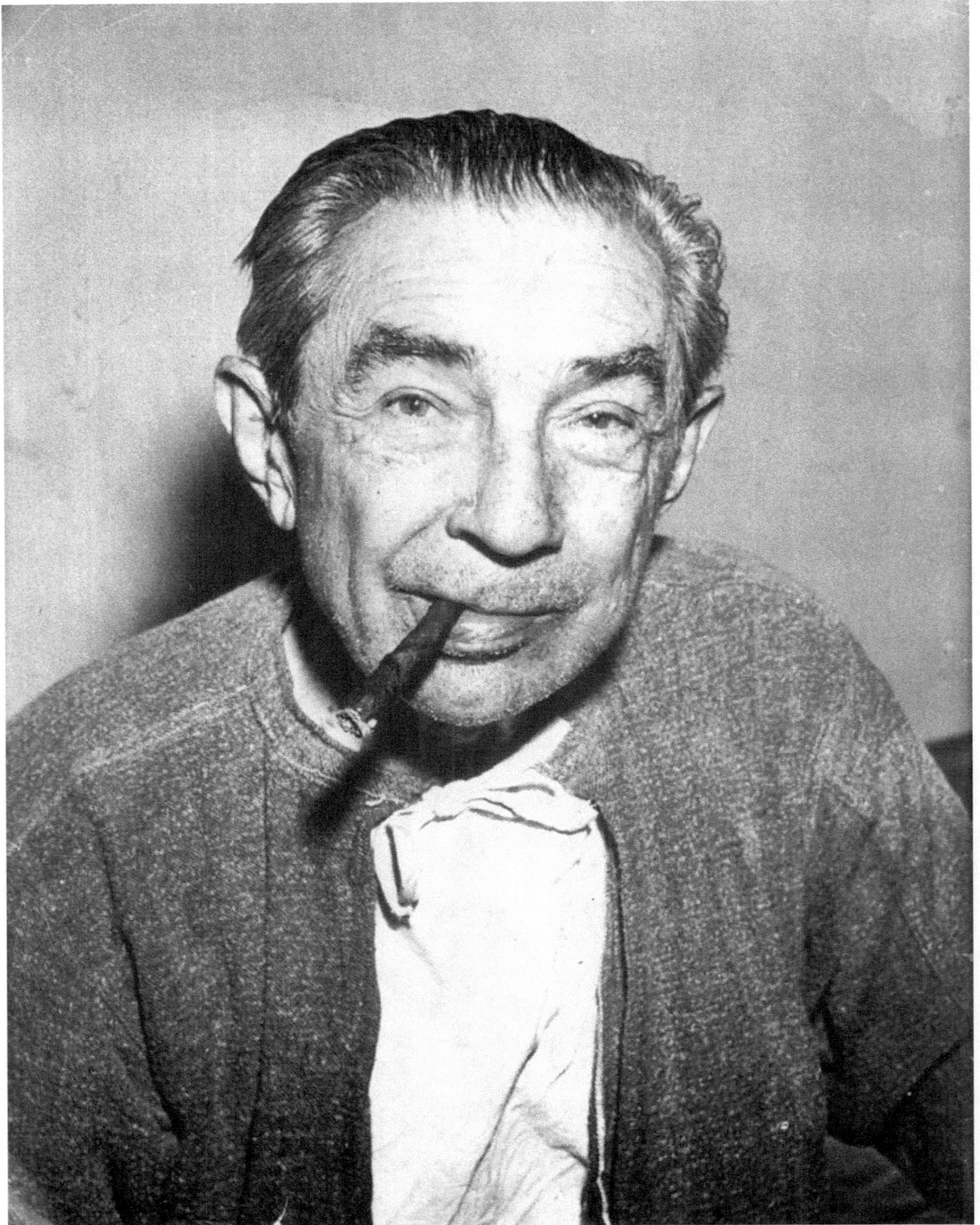

Bela, shortly before his death, enjoying a De Nobili King.

29. Married? *Yes*   Or want to be?_____ To whom?_____

    Date *Jan. 31- 1933*   Children?_____

    Favorite type of man or woman *Reserved and Honest*

30. What do you do for diversion and recreation aside from sports?
    (Dance, sing, write, paint, compose music, sclup, read, games) –

    _____

31. Where do you prefer to live permanently?
    (Seashore, mountains, city, abroad)_____

32. Where do you live now? (Apartment, House, seashore, city,

    mountains?)_____

33. Where have you traveled? *All over the world*

34. Who are your closest friends? *Stage Hands*

35. What makes you angry? *Talk*

36. What pets have you? *3 Dogs*

37. What do you do on the set? *Smoke*

38. Where do you go week-ends? *Outing*

39. Do you own any cars, airplanes, yachts, horses? *Car*

40. Interested in politics? *Yes*

41. Pet peeves *Aggravation*   Live with parents? *No*

42. Pet economy *Matches + Corks*   Pet extravagance *Old Wines and Good Cigars*

43. Favorite dress _____   Favorite perfume *Eau de Cologne*

44. DO YOU SMOKE? *Yes*   Speak any foreign language? *Hungarian and others*

45. Your greatest thrill *When I got aboard ship to come to America*

46. DO YOU LIKE

    Autographs? *No*   Rain? *No* To write letters? *No*

    Night clubs? *No*   Animals *Yes* To pose for stills *No*

    Street cars? *No*   Children *Yes*   To carry umbrellas *No*

    Prohibition? *No*   Sun baths? *Yes* Showers or bathtubs *both*

    To entertain *Yes* Fan mail *Yes*   Modern architecture *Yes*

    To sleep late? *Yes*   Holidays *?*   Personal appearances *No*

    Silk underwear *No*   Premiers *No* To drive your own car *No*

    Radio programs *No*   To dine at home *Yes* Open cars *No*

    To go shopping? *Yes* Airplanes *No* To read before sleeping *Yes*

    Ice cream cones *No*   Bathsalts *No*   Letters of introduction?

    No To travel alone? *Yes* Hollywood *Yes* Bright or subdued colors

MODEL: CARMEN W.

ElishaC Photography

WWW.ELISHAC.WEBS.COM
ELISHACPHOTOGRAPHY@GMAIL.COM

THE

OTHER

VAMPIRES

Bela Lugosi wasn't the only classical horror star to indulge in the snuff habit. Almost all of the early vampire writers, actors and directors were snuff freaks. We've rounded up some of the known snuffers, though at times information is a bit scant regarding their preferences. A big thanks for this article goes out to Todd Woodruff, who operates the Hollywood Museum in Santa Monica and collects props and trinkets from so-called 'B' film actors and productions of bygone years.

James Malcolm Rymer

Little is known about JM Rymer (1814-1884), the Scotsman that (allegedly) wrote the first modern vampire thriller, 1847's *Varney the Vampire*, a serialized "Penny Dreadful" that served as a partial inspiration to Bram Stoker's later *Dracula*.

References to snuff abound in Rymer's writings, including an autobiographical essay in which he confesses a love for perfumed French Snuff.

Sheridan Le Fanu

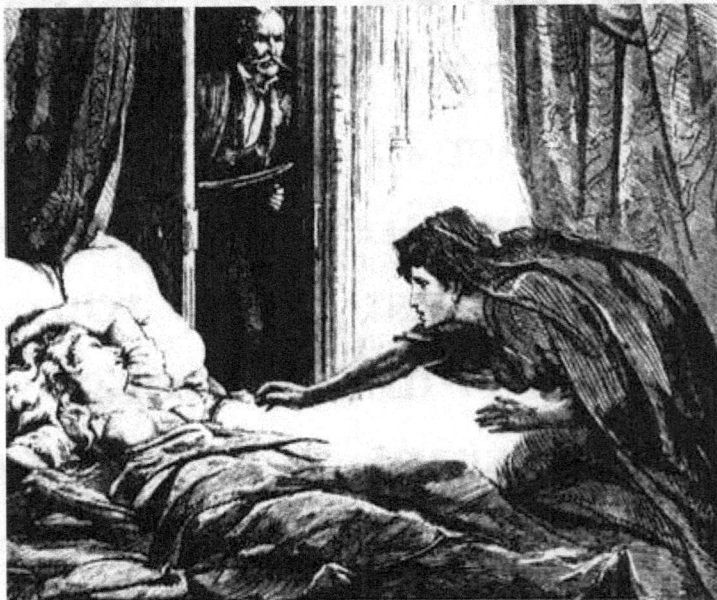

Joseph Thomas Sheridan Le Fanu (1814-1873) wrote hundreds of short stories, articles, essays and novels within his lifetime, and it's hard not to find a reference to snuff in almost every one. This comes as no surprise, as the man himself reportedly used a half a pound a day!

His 1872 novella *Carmilla*, about a lesbian vampire, is one of the most important works in the literary vampire genre and was perhaps the biggest single influence on Stoker's *Dracula,* as well as Henry James' *Turn of the Screw*. Every sexy vampress that has ever donned a skimpy outfit and fed on another buxom, willing female victim owes her existence to Carmilla.

Bram Stoker

Irish-born Abraham Stoker (1847-1912) probably did more to popularize the myth of the modern vampire than any other single person.

Almost a decade in the making, 1897's Dracula set the stage for basically every vampire story to come for the next 100 years. Stoker claimed that his inspiration for the novel came one night after a large lobster dinner and a heaping helping of Lundyfoot Snuff caused him to have a nightmare about an "aristocratic" man chasing him through the woods, attempting to drain him of his blood.

One of Stoker's paper maché snuffboxes was auctioned off by Sotheby's in the 1950's for a then-astounding price of $5,000. (In comparison, his cigar cutter sold for less than half of that sum!)

Rudyard Kipling

Joseph Rudyard Kipling (1865-1936), famous for works such as *The Jungle Book* and the epic poem *Gunga Din*, used snuff daily and died owning an impressive collection of Chinese snuff bottles and ornate snuffboxes. Many of the characters in his stories also used snuff.

Kipling's 1898 poem *The Vampire* was written in a "white flash" after viewing the eponymously named painting by Philip Burne Jones (right). (*See the Theda Bara entry for more information.*)

81

Häxan: Witchcraft Through The Ages

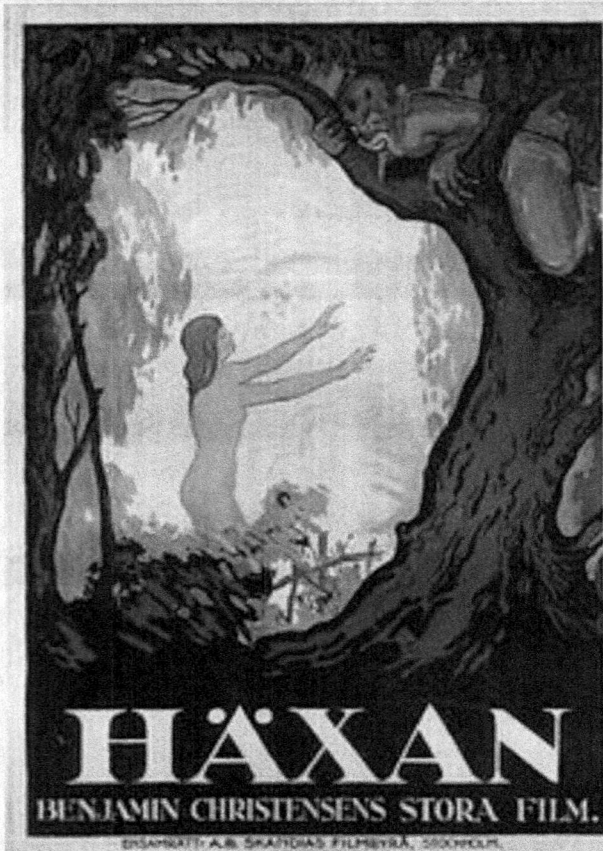

Almost everyone involved in the Danish/Swedish production of 1922's *Häxan,* a documentary concerning satanism, was a user of nasal snuff or oral snus. From directors Benjamin Christensen and Johan Ankerstjerne, to composer Launy Grøndahl, to stars Oskar Stribolt and Clara Pontoppidan, one can only imagine the amount of snus that flowed during the production of this landmark film.

The film was banned in many countries due to its graphic depictions of horror, nudity, sex, satanism and violence. In a foreshadowing of the controversy surrounding *The Exorcist* 50 years later, religious leaders went so far as to suggest that there was an actual satanic presence embedded within the film print itself.

The film was considered lost for many years, until a 1967 condensation entitled *Witchcraft Through The Ages* (narrated by occasional snuffer William S. Burroughs) made the midnight movie circuit and became a cult classic. A fully restored print was finally discovered and released to DVD in 2001.

Clara Pontoppidan (right, nude) recalled in her biography how one of her chores growing up was to make snus for her mother and father. "You cooked the snuff in water and potash and then added the flavorings, like juniper and lingon wild berries. Then you let it sit in the hot room in back for several days until the smell was just right. One little mistake and the whole batch would be ruined."

Gustaf Molander

Gustaf Molander (188-1973) was a Finnish-born director that later immigrated to Stockholm to make some of its earliest films. Though the snuser was never directly involved with a vampire film, he was instrumental in getting the 1922 witchcraft documentary *Häxan* (a.k.a. *Witchcraft Throughout The Ages*) distributed throughout Scandinavia. Were it not for his efforts, *Häxan* may today have been a "lost" film.

Molander was a "traditional" snuser, meaning he took it nasally as opposed to orally. In his film *Förseglade läppar* ("Lips Are Sealed") the female protagonist is asked why she uses snus nasally instead of under her lip. She replies "My nose belongs to snuff, but my mouth belongs to God."

Edward Van Sloan

Edward Van Sloan (1882-1964) was a veteran character actor who appeared in nearly all of the major Universal monster movies of the 30's and 40's. His best remembered role is as Dracula's antagonist Abraham Van Helsing in the 1931 version of *Dracula*.

Van Sloan had a great affinity for Copenhagen Snuff, which he developed as a young boy growing up in Minnesota. While living in Los Angeles, he would have his brother in Pennsylvania send him vast quantities of Copenhagen as it was then unavailable on the West Coast.

Van Helsing is saved from a certain death when he opens his giant snuffbox and Dracula is powerless to avoid taking a pinch.

Charles Ogle

Early silent film actor Charles Ogle (1865-1940) never played a vampire, but his portrayal of the Frankenstein Monster in Thomas Edison's 1910 film adaptation earned him a spot in horror history. Ogle covered himself in pounds of flour and snuff to give his monster a dusty, dirty look on film. He can also be seen snuffing in 1917's *Rebecca of Sunnybrook Farm* out of what looks to be a wooden snuff box.

Theda Bara

Theda Bara (1885-1955), nicknamed "The Vamp" or "The Vampire Lady" caused such a stir during her tenure as a star that it was rumored that she was in fact a *real* vampire. The publicity department for Fox Films went nuts with "leaked" details of her personal life, such as being a descendant of Cleopatra, sleeping in coffins (with skeletons of former lovers), having never been seen in daylight, etc. Even her name (an anagram for *"Arab Death"*) was an elaborate studio concoction. One of her bios stated that she used "Egyptian Snuff, the finest of its kind, heavily flavored with neroli. It's [sic] box is made from precious gold and rupees." Whether this was true, or just another studio fabrication is hard to discern.

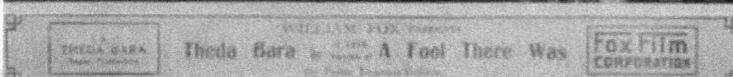

But Thedosia Goodman (her given name) does have the distinction of being the very first movie vampire ever. She played "The Vampire" in 1915's *A Fool There Was*, which was based on Rudyard Kipling's poem *The Vampire*. Her scenes (**left**), like Kipyard's poem, were heavily influenced by Philip Burne-Jones' 1897 painting *The Vampire* which graces the cover of this month's issue.

Max Schreck & F.W. Murnau

Both the star (above) and director (right) of 1922's silent German Expressionist film *Nosferatu* were veteran snuff users. Actor Max Schreck (1879-1936) was an eccentric loner who carried a birchbark snuff box on his person and spent a lot of time sleeping in the Black Forest. In one film, 1923's *Die Straße* ("The Street"), his blind character can be seen taking a pinch of snuff from a sympathetic young boy.

Schreck **was** the original film Dracula. Even though the character's names and some plot details were altered, Bram Stoker's widow successfully sued the makers of *Nosferatu* for copyright infringement and all copies of the film were ordered to be destroyed. This greatly angered director Murnau (1888-1931), who considered *Nosferatu* to be his life's masterpiece (along with his 1926 adaptation of *Faust*.) He immigrated to the US shortly after and died in a car crash.

During the peak of his success in Germany, Murnau was said to be a daily visitor to the Pöschl Snuff factory, where he would arrogantly fill his snuffbox and walk out without paying for it, or even acknowledging the people inside the store. Thankfully, both *Nosferatu* and Pöschl remain intact today.

Tod Browning

The famed director of 1931's *Dracula* (pictured here offering a Lucky Strike to Lon Chaney) was himself a chain smoker, but would resort to chewing tobacco or dipping snuff while on set, as early film cameras were highly sensitive to smoke. (Chaney incidentally smoked a whopping **four packs** a day.)

Chaney, not Lugosi, was Browning's first choice to play Dracula, but tragically Chaney would die of throat cancer during pre-production, paving the way for Lugosi's breakthrough. Tod Browning was so despondent over the death of Chaney that he rarely appeared on set, leaving most of the direction to cinematographer Karl Freund.

Ironically, Browning himself would succumb to throat cancer in 1962, having most of his throat, neck and tongue removed before finally passing away at age 82.

After *Dracula*, his most well known film was perhaps 1932's *Freaks*, which featured live circus "freakshow" actors in starring roles. The film was banned upon release and didn't garner a cult following until the 1960's, when the fully uncensored version was finally re-released theatrically. (See next issue's *Strange...But True* column for more info on *Freaks*.)

Carl Theodor Dreyer

Carl Dreyer (1889-1968) was a Danish director famous for his love of snus. Now recognized as one of history's great directors, his crowning achievement (1932's *Vampyr*) was released to mixed reviews but is now regarded as one of the best films of its era.

At the time of his death, Dreyer was working on a biographical film about Jesus. Rumor has it that he was buried with a can of his beloved Ettan snus.

CARL THEODOR DREYER'S
VAMPYR

"Every scene feels like a waking nightmare."
1932's Vampyr.

John Carradine

John Carradine (1906-1988) appeared in more movies than any other major actor in American cinema. He played Dracula several times, on stage as well as in *House of Dracula* (1945), in which his performance was at that time the closest to Stoker's own description of Dracula in his novel.

Carradine was a classically trained Shakespearean actor, and before each stage performance, he would "set the mood" by shaving by candlelight with a straight razor, killing all electrical lights, and shunning his cigarettes for a perfumed snuff, all actions that "sent him back in time" so he could better understand his character's mood and motivations.

Boris Karloff

Karloff the Mummy, trying to decide whether he's in the mood for a pipe, a cigar, or a bit of snuff.

Boris Karloff, real name Bill Pratt (1887-1969) was, like Lugosi, a true connosieur of fine tobacco.

After the British-born actor toiled away in Hollywood for several years, his big break finally came when Lugosi opted out of *Frankenstein* in 1931 and Karloff won the title role. He left an impressive body of work before his death of pneumonia brought on from complications from emphysema.

Whether his tobacco in was a pipe, a cigarette, a cigar, or even a hookah (!), Karloff delighted in smoking it. He also used snuff occasionally (preferring the Wallflower flavor), and had a pewter snuffbox initialed "BK", a gift from James Whale.

Always the consummate gentleman, whenever Karloff was in the company of females, he would politely ask permission to smoke his pipe. If he was in a snuffing mood, he would take out his snuffbox, rap it twice with his knuckles, and offer it to anyone around before taking a pinch. He once claimed that the snuff greatly helped his rheumatoid arthritis, which later left him confined to a wheelchair for the last few years of his life.

Basil Rathbone & Peter Lorre

Not much is known about the snuffing habits of the two veteran suspense stars Basil Rathbone (left) and Peter Lorre (right), other than they both listed snuffbox collections in their wills. If anyone has anymore information about these snuffbox collections, please write us and give us some more info.

Patrick Wymark

Character actor Patrick Wymark (1926-1970) appeared in countless films, among them the Hammer horror films of the 50's and 60's. In almost every Hammer film Wymark made, his character snuffs to an almost comical excess.

He is perhaps best known for his role in Roman Polanski's Repulsion (1969) as the psychotic landlord that demands payment (in the form of sex) from Catherine Deneuve.

Darby Jones

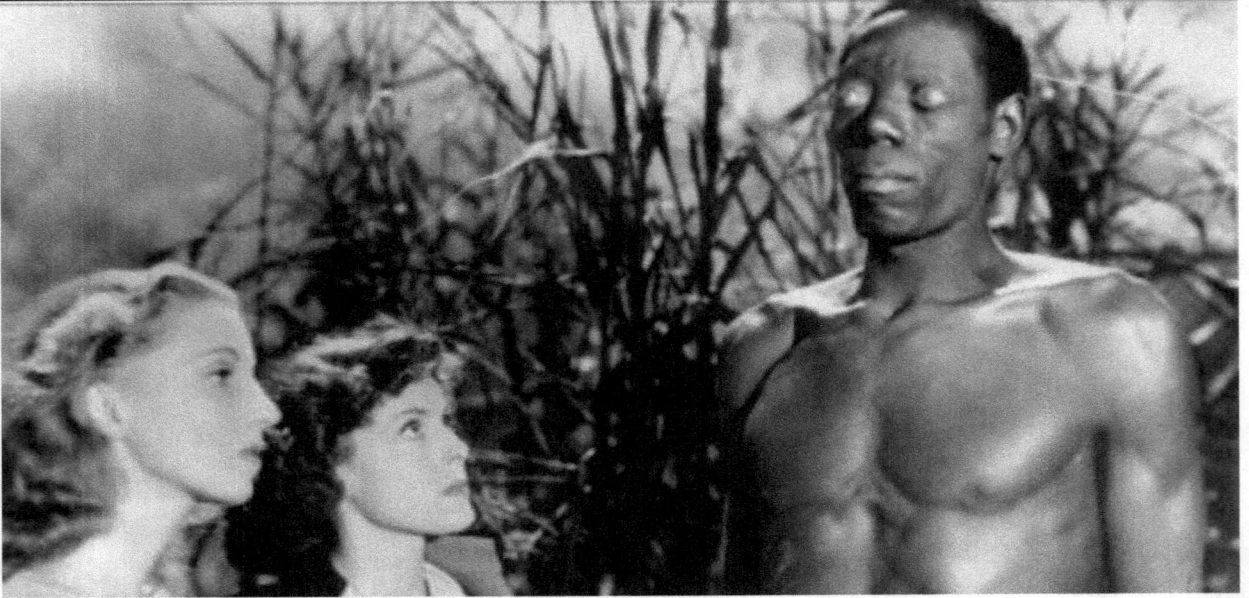

Darby Jones (1910-1986) was a veteran Hollywood performer by the time he retired in 1957 in order to open his own car garage. Though he was fortunate enough to break out of the Step n' Fetchit-type roles that plagued so many black actors of the day, he was never able to avoid the typecasting as the "African Chief" or "restless native" in B-movie adventures or poorly-made *Tarzan* sequels.

He's best remembered today as the "lead" zombie in Val Lewton's surrealistic *I Walked With a Zombie* (1943). His piercing eyes and giant, gaunt frame so impressed Lewton that he cast Jones without having him read a line of the script.

According to his relatives, Darby used about a tin of Dental Snuff every two days. He is sorely missed.

Peter Cushing & Christopher Lee

The quintessential Van Helsing and Dracula. Peter Cushing (left, 1913-1994) and Christopher Lee, (right, 1922-present) made almost twenty horror films together, usually with Lee as Dracula and Cushing portraying Van Helsing.

Both men were fond of smoking, Cushing preferring the pipe while Lee preferred cigars. But they also shared a love for snuff, which Cushing switched to in the early 80's after being diagnosed with prostate cancer. He was told that smoking would worsen his condition, but in his own words "The old boy [Doctor] never said anything about snuff!" He lived another 12 years after his diagnosis.

Lee can occasionally be seen taking snuff in some of his non-Dracula films for Hammer. It is unclear whether he still uses tobacco today (at age 91) but he's still active in films, specifically vampire horror pictures. He just shot a small cameo for director Tim Burton's *Dark Shadows* remake.

Barry Atwater

If your television was turned on January 11, 1972, chances are it was tuned to ABC, where Dan Curtis (of Dark Shadows fame) had created what would become the most widely viewed TV movie of all time, *The Night Stalker*.

The plot followed bumbling reporter Carl Kolchack (Darren McGavin) as he tries to pull the lid off a serial killer who has been draining Las Vegas showgirls of their blood. He eventually runs into vampire Janos Skorzeny, played by the brilliant Barry Atwater (1918-1978).

Atwater had a long career in stage dramas, but would turn to television work (which he felt was often subpar) when he needed money. His fellow actors described him as an eccentric, exceedingly kind man who used dry snuff and would always carry around a notebook with him, to jot down off-the-cuff poems and notes. We plan to run some of Barry's snuff poetry in a future issue, along with a feature article about him that will go into more detail about his life.

Roberts Blossom

Roberts Blossom (1924-2011) could have almost been the flip side to the same coin that featured Barry Atwater. A talented stage actor, playwright and poet, Blossoms rarely made theatrical films unless he was in need of money.

Born in New Haven, Connecticut and raised in Asheville, NC, he left school there to attend Harvard in hopes of becoming a therapist. He was then drafted into the Army during WWII, but he claimed "conscientious objector" status and spent the remaining six weeks of his military career in the Psyche Ward.

He began acting in several plays (even appearing once as Dracula, though in this version of the story, God takes pity on Dracula and releases him from his vampiric curse. Dracula goes on to try and help humanity, but they shun him because he's an ex-vampire). In the fifties, he started writing his own plays and began self-publishing his poetry, winning several prestigious awards.

The 70's marked a turning point in his career. After appearing in the 1972 film *Slaughterhouse Five,* he was cast as Ezra Cobb in the 1974 classic *Deranged: Confessions of a Necrophile*, a film closely based on the story of the "Butcher of Plainfield" Ed Gein, the notorious cannibal killer. His sympathetic performance as a man so in love with his mother that he kills other woman so his mom will have "friends to talk to" is both disturbing and unforgettable.

Listen, kid. This ride ain't gonna last. Whatever you do, DO NOT start doing heroin and tweeting about it online. You'll look stupid.

Like Atwater, he used a great deal of snuff and often wrote poems about it (many of his books are still available from second hand dealers). Modern audiences may remember him best as the creepy but lovable old man next door in 1990's *Home Alone.*

He died peacefully last year in Santa Monica, California, snuffbox in his hand and poetry book in his lap.

Klaus Kinski

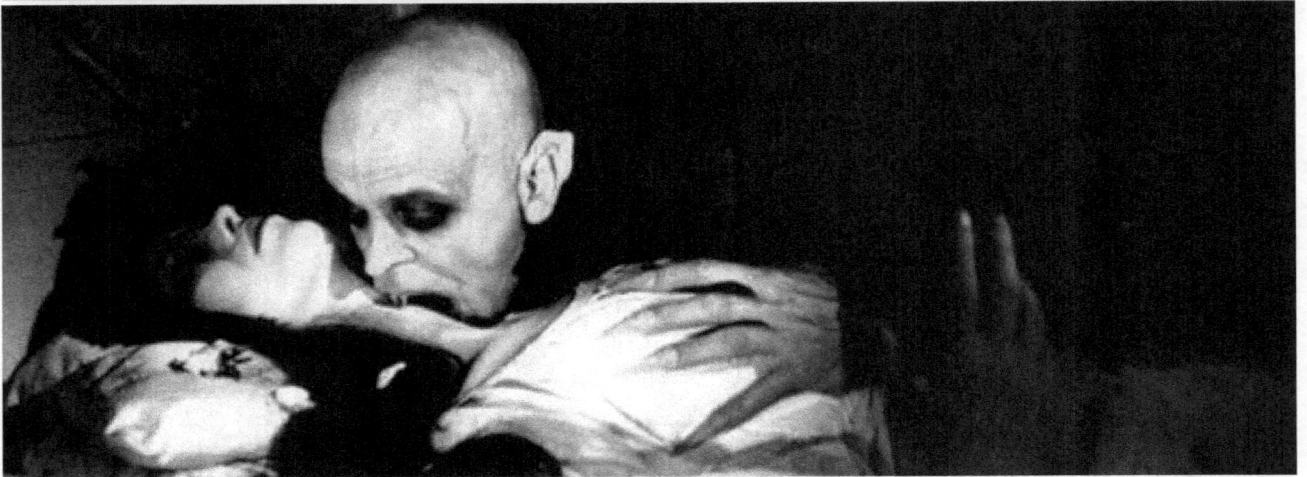

Klaus Kinski (1926-1991) was a brilliant, twisted German actor best remembered as Nosferatu in Werner Herzog's 1979 remake and for 1972's *Aguirre, the Wrath of God.* He is the father of actress Natassja Kinski.

A complete anarchist, Kinski was drafted into the Nazi army in 1943 and had deserted by 1944. He was subsequently captured by the Germans and sentenced to death, but was able to escape once more and surrender to British troops. He made his acting debut in POW Camp 186 in Essex, and after the war took on as many roles in films and plays as he was offered.

In his autobiography, Kinski mentions tobacco being in such short supply during the War. "There were no cigarettes to be had, no cigars," he claimed. "Only snuff. Snuff, snuff snuff. Oh, how I loathed snuff. But today, I still get the odd itch for it and buy a packet, to remind me of the "good times" in Bavaria bleeding to death from a British shot to the arm."

Udo Kier

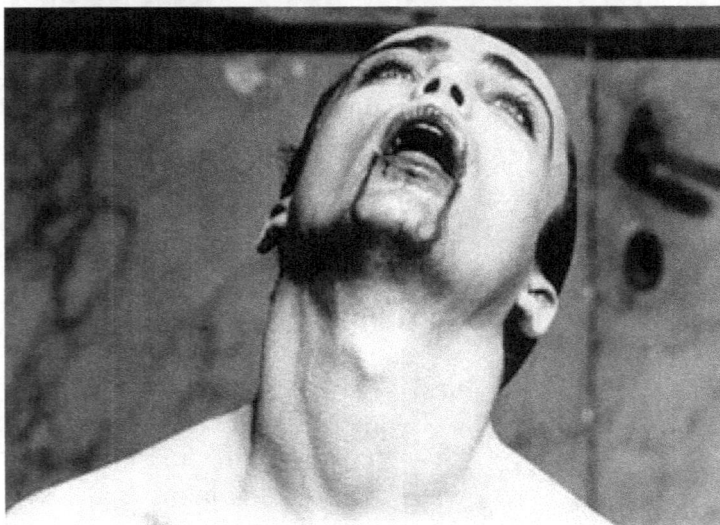

The German born Kier (1944-present), whom Crimson Paige has described as the "sexiest man that ever walked the face of the earth" has appeared in hundreds of films, tv shows, plays, music videos and video game roles.

He has at least a dozen vampire films to his credit, among them *Andy Warhol's Dracula* and the *Blade* series.

Still in high demand as an actor today, he has been ocassionally spotted using Wilsons of Sharrow snuff. (Though raised in Germany, Udo has lived in England since age 16).

Sean Bean

Sean Bean, dedicated nasal snuffer, has appeared in dozens of Hollywood blockbusters, including *The Lord of the Rings* trilogy.

He can be currently caught in the HBO series *Game of Thrones* battling Ice Vampires and other strange mythological beasts of prey.

Brett Cullen

Currently on the big screen in *The Dark Knight Rises*, Cullen is a former dipper who has recently switched to Swedish snus. His brand? Onyx, of course.

Catch him in the recent TV show *The Gates* to see him deal with the business affairs of an entire cast of supernatural beings, including his vampire wife Vanessa.

Alexander Skarsgård

Alexander Skarsgård (son of famous character actor Stellan Skarsgård, right) are both fans of General snus. The elder Skarsgård is rumored to prefer the loose while the younger is all about the portions.

Skarsgård portrays 1100-year old viking vampire king Erik Northman on the hit HBO series *True Blood*. His father was asked to join the cast but was too busy with the recent *Thor* and *Avengers* movies.

Honorable Mention:
Brad Pitt

Whether he's chewing or dipping tobacco (*Moneyball*), sniffing snuff (*Inglorious Basterds*) or smoking (take your pick), Brad Pitt has used a *lot* of tobacco on film. Rumors abound regarding whether or not he really used snuff in *Inglorious Basterds* or if he was just "play acting". Rumor also has it that he's used Swedish snus in real life to quit smoking. Who knows? We tried to ask his mom and all we got was a diatribe about Obama this and gay marriage that. But what's important is that he played a vampire one time, along with that lunatic Tom Cruise way back in *Interview With A Vampire*.

We hope you've enjoyed this somewhat unusual foray into our celluloid past. Many people forget that at one time, snuffing was just as common as smoking, and many of the past masters we see on screen were as enthusiastic about the stuff as we are today.

If you have any information about any of the actors featured in this article regarding their snuff habit, please send it in to us so we can add it to the archives. Much of what we have to go on is hearsay and rumor, or seventy year old press kits that may or may not be accurate. We'd like to once again thank Todd Woodruff and Angela Jones for their help with this article.

STE

Sheffield Stories

By
Gillian Bromley

I think a lot of you will want to know about the actual process of the manufacturing of the snuff that was made at Wilsons. Initially I wasn't involved in the process but later on my role was key in the day to day running of the mill.

I was given a new role when our cashier left, this meant the daily processing of all the cheques and bookkeeping and eventually this led to me working with the accountant and being involved in the daily processes of the mill.

Everything would of course start with the leaf. My job was to order leaf from head office. All of it was coded, some I can remember, like MNFL4F from Malawi. We also purchased leaf from Canada and the USA. At the end of every month I would do what was called 'throughput accounts' which started right with the leaf and ended with the finished goods on the shelf in the stores. I had to ensure each part of the process was balanced and that the by-product of one process went on to the next and it all added up properly. I could then produce the profit and loss manufacturing account so we could see how things were looking financially. It took me a long time to be confident at this, and I hated doing it initially as it would take me about 10 days to do a "month's end" account. Eventually I had it down to three days' work which I looked forward to doing.

So to start with, the leaf arrived in huge cases on a lorry and was unloaded with a hoist. The hoists had chains which lifted the cases onto wheeled trollies. I often used to have a go with the push button electrics if I happened to be walking across the yard when a delivery was being unloaded. This process took a good while and required most of the staff to manage it. I liked the way I could make the cases go up and down in the air with the control pad. Ooooohhh, the power!

We had an accountant who I worked closely with. He couldn't understand why there were such losses at the end of the month with the leaf that we had in stock - then we realised that as the leaf was stored it actually lost weight due to the water evaporating from it, so we came to understand exactly why there were such losses every month.

Each leaf would be different. For example, those with a lot of stem didn't lose as much moisture. The recipes involved leaves in a ratio of differing quantities for various flours as we called them, the amount of stem and differing colours of leaves gave varying textures to the end result. Country of origin would be taken into consideration along with colour and the way the leaf had been cured. The leaves were tightly packed into the cases and the aromatic smell was heady on the floors where it was stored. Given the huge amount of tobacco available from all around the world, the number of flours that we made, and the infinite amounts of flavouring used in the process, it was a safe prediction that even the most cultured of noses could not counterfeit our snuffs!

The bales would be passed through the wooden floors in the olden days by the hoist and chains, until they reached the floor where they were stored or used. These were huge trapdoors with metal rings, I can remember the floorboards were very broad and were well worn; some even had slight gaps in them so you could see the light coming from the floor below. In more recent days a lift was installed with rolling metal doors which was a bit hit and miss; occasionally I would travel in the lift to save me running up all the wooden stairs to the top floor and the men would fool around pretending the lift had got stuck so for the most part I would have to walk!

The leaf was put through a huge threshing machine on the top floor which would break the leaves by a rotor tooth mechanism into small particles. This was an incredibly dusty job and I would often see one of the men wearing a mask and getting really dusty in the process. After this the mix of leaves would be fed into the atomizing grinding mill. After grinding, salts and minerals were added along with water- 12% of each to every 400 pound batch of the flour. This then went into the 'dressing' machine which was like a fine sieve where only the finest of particles passed through, the dressed snuff was then kept in huge oak barrels and left to mature until it was needed in the mixing process. On the side of the barrels they wrote in chalk which flour it contained and the weight inside the barrel. Thinking back, the men used to roll the barrels on their edges to move them around; Health and Safety would never allow that these days.

I can remember sticking my head into those huge barrels which stored the finished snuff, especially if I had a cold. Incidentally, not many people in the mill ever had colds. I wonder if it was due to the camphor? I don't know! After the mill closed, those oak barrels that had stored 1000's of pounds of snuff during their working life were sold to any employee who wanted them, the biggest were of course massive and of no use to anyone, but the smaller ones were good if sawn in half and used as flower or plant containers. (That was if they stayed together, as sawing them in half weakened them and they would fall apart. I remember that they cost £5 each!)

So after this process came the flavouring of the snuff, a closely guarded secret. I can tell you that part of my role was to make out the mixing cards for each day. Mr Bamber, the mill manager (a true gentleman who I became very fond of) would phone me and ask to deliver the mixing cards according to his instructions. These were made out on long thin strips of grey card which I would take into the mill and leave for the workers; they then made each mix up accordingly. We had a flavour room where all the various bottles were stored on dusty shelves, the more expensive ones in tiny glass bottles, our most expensive essential oil was attar of roses which cost £124 per fluid ounce (back in the 80's) and only one or two drops were added to each recipe where needed. We had huge cans of menthol crystals (I think they came from China) and these were melted in hot water and added to the mix, the smell was incredibly strong and would make your eyes water! We also used camphor, bergamot, and wallflower to name a few.

My job was also to stocktake and order essential oils and flavours each month. When the flavour orders arrived Mr. Bamber would bring the bottles in to me and put a small amount of flavour on a strip of paper and ask me to guess what it was. Some were easy, the bergamot and lemony ones, others not so. I learned that different liquids of flavour had different weights so when it came to stocktaking I had to use a conversion calculation so they all were uniform weights; some were in drams- an old fashioned liquid measurement, hard to explain really!

So, after the flours were mixed with the concoction of flavours, they became 'finished snuff' and waited until they were needed in the packing rooms, they were also stored in the oak barrels to be taken to the packing rooms where the ladies used huge scoops to tip the snuff into the machines where they were filled and lidded. After this they were packed into the various containers, i.e., pocket boxes which held around 8g and these came off the production line at around 2 per second, 50,000 boxes per day. They were then overwrapped with cellophane window paper.

Sheffield at Sunrise.

The final step was to place them in cartons of 24.

Ever so often the ladies from the mill would come over to the office with their machine check weighing cards. I then performed a complex calculation which enabled me to see that the right amount of snuff had been used in the processes for that day- different size tins had different calculations and I got to know by just looking at the cards in the end! Some were filled by hand, like the 1/2 and 1lb drums we sold. Then, as they were packaged, a label was stuck on the side which had the date coded into it so we could tell what date it was packed. Some tobacconist shops sold it loose by the ounce, as we used to supply little cone shaped bags for the retailer to dispense it in. (How cute!)

The mill employees always seemed to do the same role, day in and day out. There was no real mix of roles; some women would work all their days and years on the same machinery, and the men would have the same tasks to perform each day. I remember the foreman who did the mixing and flavouring constantly smelled of menthol crystals-I bet his whole house smelled of them!

Some of the roles we had were specific. We had a caretaker's cottage on site and he also worked in the mill; there was the storekeeper who maintained and took care of all the packaging materials; there were the girls who mainly worked on the machinery in packing, and we had a foreman and forewoman who were kind of managers over the men and women in the mill. The men wore brown overalls (I suppose because of the brown snuff!) and the engineer wore navy overalls. The women wore blue smock type overalls and Mr. Bamber wore a white coat, a bit like a doctor. Sometimes I would wear Mr. Bambers' white coat if I was working for a few hours. I felt really special and important with my jacket and clipboard, even though I really wasn't!

We also had Sales Representatives who travelled the countryside going into tobacconist stores up and down the country promoting our products. We had one to cover the south of the country and one for the north. I used to dread them coming into the office because it meant that they brought back store returns. We had this policy of sale or return, so if a product just did not sell they could return it for full credit. I would then spend hours at my desk calculating how many tins of each they had sent back by counting out the tins. The tins would be then broken down and emptied by the workers; I often used to see them placed in a circle with baskets full of pocket boxes being painstakingly emptied.

The snuff, as it was old, would be recycled and re-flavoured, as anything over three months old would have lost its flavour. Apart from airtight tins, I spent many a day lining them up on my desk seeing if they could go back into stock. Each one was tapped by my pencil, and depending on the sound I could tell if the seal had broken, in which case they would be broken down and recycled, which was a pretty simple routine except if you had a couple of hundred to do. Then it was a very boring task. Our head office at Ogden's would also send in their returns, and my heart would sink when they'd bring me 5 or 6 massive boxes full of every type of snuff. Many were broken and I would always get covered in the stuff. My desk had a green leather top (posh, eh?) and it was always orange by the time I was done. Wiping it made it worse and everything got covered, so eventually I donned my white coat and took to sorting in the mill to make my life easier, though it wasn't as white by the time I was finished, more like orange!

I often went home reeking of snuff or cigarette smoke as in the 80's it was OK to smoke in the workplace, I think I must have passively smoked for years being having sat next to smokers for several years. Smoking was in fact encouraged, as Imperial Tobacco gave us a cigarette allowance of 200 cigarettes per month. My job was to order for the employees and distribute every 4 weeks, so you can imagine how popular I was on a Friday afternoon handing out the allowances! I personally never smoked, but sold mine very cheaply and I saved the money towards Christmas presents. What a good girl I was!

STE

*What a good girl Gill **still is** for writing a column for us every issue! Her years of experience at the J&H Wilson plant are fascinating to our readers and we hope that she continues to share her unique perspective with us.*

"A Brit By Any Other Name"

A Winifred Skinny Misadventure by
Micah Rimel

Photography by Elisha Cozine
Model: Jordyn Ballentine

"Bugger this!" The pallid Englishman expostulated as he fought to stay seated upon the wide and tightly cinched saddle atop his lethargic and determinedly narcoleptic mule.

"Uh, yeah," Drawled Winifred Skinny, snuff courier extraordinaire, as he witnessed his companions struggle with the stationary beast. "They can be real tough to mount when they're all still and calm like that." His words brought forth badly muffled chuckles and snide snickers from the growing crowd of onlookers. The Englishman missed the snub, so absorbed was he in remaining perched upon the solid unwavering creature.

"Yep. It's a real chore to hang on that ol' saw-horse, ain't it feller?" Quipped some yokel between spurting gouts of plug tobacco juice from between his remaining half dozen yellow teeth. More chuckling and even outright guffaws issued from the crowd. This was high entertainment. Even the snake oil salesman and a whole Gypsy caravan had put aside their day's busqing for a gander at this rare sight. The Englishman flopped around for a few moments more before tumbling headlong onto the muddy street. The crowd was in hysterics now, tears of mirth, guffaws of deep belly-rumbling laughter filled the vista along the street front. Winifred could not resist.

"Well I'll be! I never saw the *man* who could buck a *mule!*" The crowd roared its approval and amidst much back slapping and hoarse laughter, the mule's late rider glared at them all as he tried, and failed, to maintain his dignity while remounting.

"This calls for a pinch o' the good stuff." Winifred thought as he dug one meaty paw into the depths of his vest to retrieve Martha, his favorite horn-crafted snuff box. "Ahhhh..." he sighed after imbibing a mighty pinch, "Time to move this cargo out, master English equestrians included." He glanced disdainfully at his erstwhile companion who was busy further entertaining the populace by managing to fall a second time, against all odds, into the horse trough. Winifred sighed again. "It's gonna be a long trip. A long trip indeed."

"Quit horsing around, man!" Winifred said, annoyed enough to forget the humor implicit in the statement. The crowd applauded. Winifred's lean, muddied and bedraggled foreign friend had managed to precariously mount his beast and at a whistle from Winifred, the caravan of two took off.

Despite a false start initiated by yet another pratfall from Britain's finest, the convoy moved on nevertheless, leaving behind a pleased and mirth-filled crowd and containing a huge grinning fat man and his muddy, muttering companion. Comedians and news-men and folks who enjoyed a good laugh would repeat the tale of their departure far and wide for days and weeks to come. Even Winifred couldn't help but chuckle quietly to the recent memory as his poor bow-backed horse trudged along under its cumbersome burden. Winifred glanced back at his charge from the Empire and shook his head; recalling as he did so the circumstances that had brought them all together.

Hellwig McDougal-Barfknecht, the Scotch-Irish/Prussian mogul of the Tennessee snuff mills, had personally requested that Winifred escort his honored guest, Lord Pomfrey Sisyphus Tweedlebaron, along a typical snuff delivery into the not-so-wilds of civilized Texas. Apparently, Lord Tweedlebaron was some sort of dignitary when it came to matters pertaining to the European tobacco market, being a big-time trader and connoisseur in his own right. According to the lengthy letter of commendation, Lord Tweedlebaron had, in his travels betwixt the continents, traversed the Sahara with a band of Bedouins and taught them geometry and marksmanship (as well as how to properly hold a teacup, the pinky-less savages), not to mention his trials in New Guinea wherein he converted the entire Noaheedinnit tribe to Unitarianism and replaced their cannibalistic rituals with a formalized English breakfast. Winifred hoped the proof was in something far removed from the pudding because he doubted the man's credentials not in the least, but rather entirely. Winifred pitied the Lordling's mount almost as much as himself.

Just a few miles farther on Winifred's ears, which were finely tuned to the myriad tones of the wilderness, detected a faint high-pitched squeaking sound behind him. His honed sense didn't register it as some latent sissy-bird or castrated chipmunk so the source must be something manmade. He shifted his heavy bulk in his saddle and glared at the Englishman.

"What in the Hell is that racket?" He demurely inquired. The Englishman shrugged and said simply, "It is my snuff-box. I'm having a devil of a time unscrewing the lid. I thought a pinch might be just the ticket, what?" Winifred dismounted with a monumental grunt and sauntered over to help Lord Tweedlebaron. The moment Winifred was near the horse the Englishman crowed, "I've got it!" and a cloud of fine British snuff fill the air. The atmosphere was rent with the violent explosions of man and horse resoundly sneezing alike. Lord Tweedlebaron's horse reared and flung his meager hooves in the air. One particular flying hoof was enough to send Winifred to the ground however. The English Lord fought his horse to a standstill before dismounting casually and crouching close to the downed and wounded Winifred's face.

"My word! Are you injured badly?" He asked, not unkindly.

"Well," Winifred coughed, "I'm not too bad personally, but..." He broke off to hack brown slugs of not too disgusting slimy phlegm created from a week's dose of British snuff onto the dusty ground. "I don't much like that a-rattlin' sound comin' from those bushes near my feet!" He continued, a little breathlessly and perspiring with a volume born of both primal fear and fried-chicken induced obesity.

"Oh!", exclaimed Lord Tweedlebaron. "There? In these bushes?" The English lord began thwacking aimlessly into the brush.

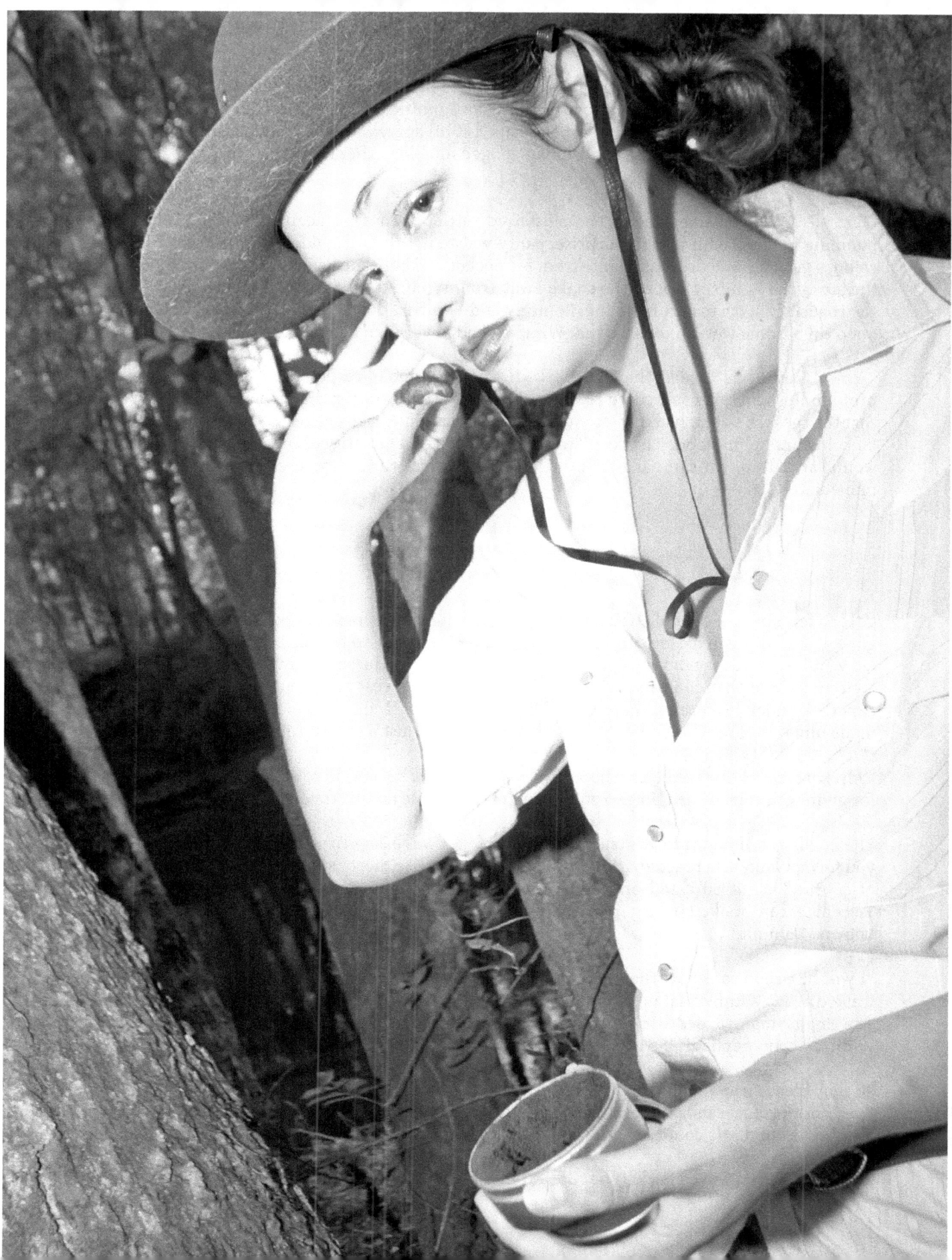

"NO!" Screamed Winifred, "It's a dang rattler, you fool, watch out!" The warning went unheeded and the British dignitary flushed an eight foot rattler from sunning on the side of the road. And as it turned out, he was much less than happy. The serpent leaped at his aggressor, hell bent on death and destruction (and maybe a light snack later). The Englishman dodged nimbly to the side with a quickness born of a man bred to avoid the leprous poor of London.

"@#$%!" Winifred screamed as the plus-sized rattler's fangs bit deep and the serpent's venom began pumping home. To his utmost surprise, panty-waist English lord suddenly seemed to grow a huge pair of cojones grandes and drew and knife from his pocket and beheaded the ornery beast. Blood fountained in the air as the Pomfrey ripped the snake away from Winifred's leg and dragged the huge man away from the roadside. With expert handling, Pomfrey laid Winifred down, turniqueted his affected leg and pulled out a tin of some wet-ish tobacco that Winifred had never seen before.

"What, *cough*, is *cough* that?" He asked. The Englishman responded, "This is Swedish Snus! A most profound product; it's salt cured tobacco, a perfect astringent for the serpents poison!" Winifred noted that the speaker's voice had transformed from that of a whiny rich privileged Englishman to that a confident Lincolnshire Robin Hood. The Lord Tweedlebaron placed a quantity of the Swedish Snus within Winifred's wound and, despite the initial discomfort, the Snus seemed to absorb a great quantity of the serpent's toxin immediately.

****

After a few hours of careful attention by his English nurse Winifred revived without issue, the toxins mostly gone, the swelling in his leg subsided and he felt he was ready to travel. Lord Tweedlebaron expeditiously led Winifred to the rendezvous point, assisted in delivering the snuff and ultimately being a decent bloke; a circumstance that confused Winifred then allowed him rest as he put the final pieces together. The expertise which his foreign charge had demonstrated, the facility in which he took charge of the situation made him reevaluate his companion; and made him feel just a touch guilty.

"Mr. Lord, sir" Winifred began, hoping he had addressed his new hero accurately, "I just want to apologize for givin' you such a hard time. You've been playin' a role all this time, haven't you? Just playing dumb?"

The English Lord nodded, "It's true my friend. I felt it was easier to go the role of the imbecile and see how you former colonists reacted." He grinned, "You react like morons for the most part, no offense intended of course." Winifred could only blink."I masqueraded as an imbecile for your sake, not mine." Lord Tweedlebaron smoked his cigarillo and, Winifred thought, appeared much cooler than anyone he'd ever known. Dammit.

"I will be proud to report that your country has less true assholes than true heroes." He grinned as he walked away. Winifred sat up in his bed, causing the springs to contemplate suicide. "Oh and by the way..." The Englishman turned back, "Your advice on horsemanship was really... *shitty*." He laughed; as did Winifred, who replied, "So is your snuff!"

"It may please you to know that my real job is as snuff procurer for Her Royal Majesty Queen Victoria, and I've chosen your brand. Congratulations." Winifred opened his eyes and tried to shout but he was unable to utter a sound. He could say only one thing... "Your horsemanship is still pretty terrible, Limey!"

The English Lord waved back as he rode off into the sunset, ungainly and a little bit lopsided.

BLACKGUARD OF THE MONTH AWARD

Honoring outstanding achievements in Anti-tobacco asshattery

Well, it was a hard choice this month. First we had Mary Bottari over at the *Huffington Post* spewing left-wing bile and reinventing the truth regarding smokeless tobacco. (If you haven't read her op-ed, it basically goes like this: all doctors, scientists and health advocates that recommend smokeless tobacco as an alternative to cigarette smoking are all part of a vast right-wing secret society that wants to poison our youth and kick our puppies.)

Then, we had the White Knights of Massachusetts who succeeded in banning smokeless tobacco sales in pharmacies for "health" and "youth" reasons. (24 hour beer and liquor sales are still permitted, though. Guess a gallon of Jack Daniels is much healthier than a can of snuff.)

And let us not forget the ongoing farce that is the FDA tobacco "trials". Just this month, a slew of studies showing all manner of smokeless tobacco as being basically harmless were barred from being entered into record because... well, the FDA hasn't really told us that part yet. But the FDA is a government agency, so I'm sure they have our best interests at heart.

But the BGoTM award is a sacred honor we give out to the stupidest, most inane drivel-mongers in the field of anti-tobacco hysteria. This month we dug down deep and found two of the most moronic liars we've seen in a while: Heather Harris of the Canton, OH rag

The Canton Rep **(right)** and Judith Coykendall, Program Manager at Seven Hills Behavioral Health of New Bedford, Mass **(left)**.

These two ladies win this month's award for the stunning article which appeared in the July 27th *Canton Rep* (viewable here:) [http://www.cantonrep.com/life/health/x181 4082323/Smokeless-tobacco-marketing-towards-tweens] in which Heather and Judy make some interesting claims.

We've printed excerpts from this piece along with editorial rebuttals presented in bold. Heather starts off by saying:

Gone are the days of the small circular tin holding chewing tobacco or dip. **(Really? The last time I was in Canton, OH I saw grocery, tobacco and convenience stores that had shelves full of them. Heck, I've got two small, circular tins in my pocket right now. But you're right, "chewing tobacco" hasn't been widely available in a small circular tin since at least the 1940's. "Dip", however, doesn't come in anything BUT small circular cans (unless you count those giant tubs of Stokers- which happen to also be circular. But I digress).**

Now there are new-shaped tins, similar to an Altoid mint box, **(I'm going to go out on a limb here and guess that she's talking about American Camel Snus. The first part of that sentence is wrong in that snuff and snus have**

traditionally come in similarly-shaped containers for hundreds of years. Before aluminum and fiberboard, they were made of steel or wood. If anything, the round cans are the "new-shaped tins" (is that even really a thing?) and the oblong containers are a throwback to the traditional designs of yore.

The second part of that sentence implies that any rectangular, metallic tin is similar to an Altoids tin. I'll admit that an Altoids tin greatly resembles a British snuff tin. Maybe it's because Altoids was invented by Smith and Co. (London), who before entering the candy business manufactured... wait for it... Nasal snuff! I wonder if way back in Georgian Era 1760, upset mothers wrote to the Smith shop demanding that they stop putting their candy mints in snuff containers, lest their children become confused and haplessly addicted to nicotine. But I digress.)

That contain nicotine-filled "mints" that are being marketed towards the younger crowd, typically children ages 11-13. (Actually, the tins contain portioned snus comprised of tobacco flavored with different ingredients; some are indeed mint-flavored. But "nicotine mints" only exist in the same fantasy world where tobacco companies continue to market to the pre-teen set. I watch *iCarly* and *Victorious* every day and have yet to see an ad for Camel Robust.)

"When you are 11, 12, 13 years old, you think 'I'll try this, how bad can it be'," said Judith Coykendall, program manager at Seven Hills Behavioral Health of New Bedford, Mass. (Unfortunately, this has been true since the dawn of time and will probably never change. But we commend you for peeing on a forest fire.)

"When you do use tobacco at an early age, you are more likely to become addicted to alcohol and cocaine later on. It opens up the addiction pathway." (This theory has been debunked by every single credible expert on the subject and to continue to profess a belief in it seriously makes me question the safety of your patients

over at Seven Hills. But kudos to you for blaming alcoholism and cocaine addiction on smokeless tobacco- seriously, we get off on that sort of thing around here.)

And it's not just nicotine mints making a presence with the tween crowd. There is chewing gum laced with nicotine (Oh, you mean the nicotine cessation gum that the FDA is forcing the public to use in lieu of safer, more effective smokeless tobacco?), *blunt cigars that are fruity flavored* (hint: all of the tobacco inside of fruit blunts ends up in the Wal-Mart parking lot in order to make room for the chronic), *electronic cigarettes and teabags kids suck on called "Snus."* (I've never met any kids that suck on snus, but that's probably because it's not sold to anyone under the age of 18. Also, for anyone under the age of forty, when you overhear your child talking about "teabagging" someone, he or she is not talking about tobacco.)

What concerns Coykendall is that the FDA has not approved these products. (Nope, but they're doing their level best to keep them out of the hands of adult consumers.) *There are no labels outlining what is in them. "We don't know the levels of nicotine in them or what chemicals exist," she said. "Its very dangerous for them to be swallowing."*

(Actually, there are labels on them outlining the ingredients. A full list of flavorings can be found on each company's website. But unlike our Swedish pals, American manufacturers have yet to start labeling the nicotine content on the smokeless products they manufacture. See, in America, "nicotine" has become a bad word and producers are scared to bandy the term about. In all of our meetings with American smokeless tobacco reps, they replace the word "nicotine" with "satisfaction", precisely to nix the kind of addiction legalese that their lawyers have instructed them to avoid. But in Sweden, you're likely to hear a tobacco exec exclaim "try this new 21mg/g Extra Strong! It'll knock you on your ass!" But I digress.)

There is documentation of students being sent

to emergency rooms after using smokeless tobacco. Symptoms in those cases included sweating, high blood pressure and nausea, Coykendall said. (We'd love to hear more about this epidemic of nicotine overdoses in teens. The only credible report that we have in our archives concerns a 14 year old lad who ate 45 pieces of FDA-approved nicotine gum and had to have his stomach pumped. I'm sure that more cases exist, and if the author or the interviewee could cite such reports, it would make their argument slightly more credible.)

Coykendall said tobacco companies are packaging these items with the intent to lure in younger customers. "They are looking for new customers and definitely gearing these products towards young kids," Coykendall said.

When giving presentations, she brings examples with her to show parents what the smokeless tobacco products look like. "Parents say if I looked into my child's backpack, I would have thought it was candy," Coykendall said. "The mints look like Tic Tacs, and the blunt cigars look like Fruit Roll-Ups." (These parents are probably stupid and have no business breeding.)

Another area that bothers Coykendall is the cost to purchase the products. "The flavored cigars are 69 to 89 cents, they are kid-price sensitive," she said. "That's less expensive than a pack of gum or a bag of chips." (Actually, at 69 to 89 cents, you're paying about 80-100% more than the cost of manufacture of these crappy cigars. Since kids can't legally buy these anyway (and most studies show that they're receiving their tobacco and alcohol through theft rather than unscrupulous merchants), then you're just forcing adult buyers to pay 2.00 for a ten cent cigar while making a huge profit for the "evil tobacco company" you long to put out of business. Altria thanks you!)

Marilyn Edge, director of the Tobacco and Alcohol Prevention Collaboration in Western Bristol County and Foxborough, Mass., gave two presentations last school year to both parents and students in area schools.

Part of her job is to bring awareness, and like Coykendall, emphasized how these new products can have lasting and addictive effects.

"These alternative tobacco products relate to other drugs and drug paraphernalia down the road," Edge said.

Relate how? Someone using nasal snuff is going to one day move to cocaine? Someone smoking a hookah will one day trade it for a crack pipe? Someone with a lip full of Copenhagen is going to replace it with meth? Sweden, a nation of snus users, hasn't all of the sudden turned into a nation of needle junkies on the corner begging for spare kroner so they can get their next fix. Hell, in every study we've ever published, smokeless tobacco users don't even graduate to CIGARETTE SMOKING, which would seem to put a nail in the coffin (no pun intended) to all of this "gateway drug" propaganda.

Both health professionals want to educate and make parents aware that these products exist and can be harmful. "They are targeting kids with flashy wrappers and fun flavors," Coykendall said. (Clearly, fun flavors like Berwick Brown and Best SP are all the rage at the local pre-schools in New England.) "It's cheaper than marijuana and easier to get than alcohol. (Since when? Pound for pound, highly-taxed premium tobacco now costs more than tax-free marijuana in most US states. Also, the most recent studies show that teens have more trouble locating tobacco than booze.) Using these products at an early age makes you more likely to develop life-long, unhealthy and dangerous addictions."

Thank you for your opinion doc, but please stick to the facts when you're discussing people's health. By trying to ban or price smokeless tobacco out of the reach of informed adult consumers, you leave them with very unhealthy options. By saying that smokeless is just as dangerous as smoking, you are leading the public to believe that they should just keep on smoking cigarettes, which will result in the death of one out of every four smokers. Please stop killing our citizens through your ignorance and lies.

STE

STRANGE... BUT TRUE !

TOBACCO-RELATED ODDITIES AND ANECDOTES

COMPILED BY DAVID THIGPEN

A Tough One to Swallow

Vancouver, Washington resident Cuitlahvac Renteria-Martinez got more than he bargained for when he hijacked a $75,000 big rig containing about $15,000 worth of tools and equipment.

Martinez spotted an idling Freightliner in a mall parking lot and knocked on the driver's door. When he got no response, he opened up the cab and put the truck into gear.

The truck's owner, who was inside the local Sears washing grease off of his hands, noticed his tuck gone and called the police. The authorities surprised the driver by telling him that they had already located his truck, less than a half a mile away. "How did you find it so quick?" the driver asked. "Because the guy that stole it called us for an ambulance," the dispatcher replied.

It seems that as soon as Martinez left the mall parking lot, he pulled his cellphone out and called a few buddies to rendezvous with him in a state park to unload the goods. As he was giving his partner directions, Martinez absentmindedly reached for the bottle of Mountain Dew in the truck's cupholder. After taking a big swig, Martinez began to choke.

He stopped the truck in the middle of a busy intersection and frantically tried to dial 911. But his friend was still connected and Martinez was unable to figure out how to switch lines, so he jumped back into the truck and used the owner's cellphone to call for help. By this time, Martinez was turning blue and gasping for air. To make matters worse, his English was so limited that it took additional time for the dispatcher to locate a Spanish translator.

EMS quickly arrived and cleared Martinez's blocked airways. The culprit was discovered when investigators examined the Mountain Dew bottle that Martinez drank from. It was full of used Skoal and spit juice. The mixture was so thick that Martinez was unable to swallow it, and it congealed inside of his throat. After being treated, he was promptly arrested and sentenced to seven years in prison.

Cuitlahvac Renteria-Martinez: a thief so stupid that this story sounds more like an Urban Legend than a true account. But we swear: it's 100% legit, esse.

Strange... But Probably NOT True

An e-Cig, of all things, is being blamed for the New Mexico wildfire that burned about a mile of woodland along the Rio Grande on June 20th.

A park employee claims he accidentally dropped his e-cig, which caused an instant brush fire that the rangers were unable to put out before it "exploded" into a wildfire.

A more likely scenario is that the employee was smoking a real cigarette (which is forbidden during wildfire season) that caused the actual fire. Blaming an e-cig would have cleared the employee of any negligence charges and allowed him to keep his job. There are no plans to press charges and the state is considering placing e-cigs in the same prohibitive ban as regular cigarettes.

James Smith, preventative fire technician at Duke University, is leaning towards the "real cigarette" theory. "The heating elements we've examined in the e-cigarette studies we've conducted never approached the Fahrenheit needed to ignite paper. It's highly doubtful, except maybe under extremely bizarre circumstances, that an e-cig could ever cause a wildfire."

Strange... But Sadly IS True

The Travis County Fire Department (Austin, TX) responded to 12 separate brush fire calls in one day, supposedly all caused by discarded cigarette butts. Thankfully no one was injured, but the Austin Police Department will issue tickets for littering to anyone they see improperly dispose of their butts. (*Ed: Had this been a story about a tragic Hookah-related fire, everyone would have thought we were making it up.*)

Cheap Chinese Lighter Kills Man

In late March, Houston TX resident Ricky Clemmer got a shocking phone call from his brother Bill. "I'm hurt," he said. "I'm all burnt. I need to go to the hospital."

When his brother arrived, all of the skin of Bill Clemmer's face and neck was practically gone, having melted off. His chest was black and charred. "I didn't know how to touch him. His skin was just hanging on him."

The MK Triple Jet Butane gas station special.

Bill died shortly after arriving at the hospital from first degree burns. He said that the Chinese-made MK Triple Jet lighter he had just bought at a convenience store exploded after he lit his cigarette and put the lighter back into his pocket.

According to the forensics team that investigated the death, the lighter had a defective seal. After it had had been lit, the defective seal allowed the butane to keep flowing. A small flame stayed lit, hidden by the wind guard. When it was placed back into his pocket, it exploded, giving him fourth degree burns.

There is no point in attempting to sue the company, as MK has no US-based presence to penalize. Critics are demanding mandatory safety guidelines to be placed on all imported and domestic lighters in order to avoid this type of accident again.

We at the *Ephemeris* would suggest a rather more practical solution to safety issues from Chinese goods: a complete and total embargo on anything made or imported from our Communist buddies.

Domestic Squabble Ends in Woman Pouring out a can of Chewing Tobacco, Stabbing Husband

On July 25th, a Vero Beach, Florida couple were almost arrested after a conflict involving a bottle of perfume and a can of chewing tobacco.

The 28 year old woman said that the father of her three children was upset with her, so he dumped a bottle of her perfume down the drain. She responded by dumping out a tin of his chewing tobacco. In retaliation, he "bum rushed" her into a wall and then slammed her into the ground.

The woman then pulled out a pocket knife and stabbed the man in the back. "Ow! You bitch!" he screamed. "Why'd you stab me in the damn back?"

Police arrived shortly after, but the couple decided not to press charges against each other. Apparently in Florida, throwing a woman on the ground, slamming her against a wall and stabbing your boyfriend in the back are not arrestable offenses.

The police report can be read below.

Indian River County Case Report
Summary

Print Date/Time:	07/25/2012 16:32	Indian River County Sheriff's Office	
Login ID:	ahatley	ORI Number:	FL0310000
Case Number:	2012-00095921		

OfficerID: dragley, Narrative
On July 23, 2012 at approximately 0830 hours I responded to 23   2nd Street S.W. in reference to a Domestic Violence with a possible stabbing. Upon arrival I made contact with Sgt. M. Pierce and he stated that he responded to the above residence in reference to a 911 hang up and when he arrived he got information that a male had been stabbed.
I then made contact with the suspect   at the above residence and she stated that she and the father of her three kids,   got into a verbal disturbance and then it got physical.   stated that   dumped out her new bottle of perfume, so she dumped out his can of chewing tobacco. She then stated that   then picked her up and slammed her to the ground and then as she was getting up,   came at her again and attempted to bum rush her. So she grabbed the first thing that she could to protect herself and it was a pocket knife and she stated that she stabbed him in the back.   wrote a written statement and it will be entered into evidence.
    was down the street and Sgt. Pierce made contact with him to get his side of the story. See Sgt. Pierce's supplement.
There were conflicting stories and we could not determine a primary aggressor so I was instructed to present the case to the State Attorney's Office. Also, the victim,   viamently refused to have   arrested. On July 24, 2012 at approximately 1145 hours I presented the case to Assistant State Attorney Patrick O'Brien. O'Brien advised that because there were no independant witnesses and the only documentation of what happened came from the possible suspect as self defense and   refused to write a statement, O'Brien advised me to get Decination of Intents from both parties. I went to the victim   and explained to him what a Declination of Intent was and he stated that he wanted to sign and not have   arrested.
I then went to   and explained to her what a Declination of Intent was and she also stated that she would sign and not have   arrested.
There is nothing further by this Deputy, this case is exceptionally cleared.

Routing:

STE

WARNING: This product is not a safe alternative to cigarettes

HAPPIER, HEALTHIER, RICHER, THINNER
(AND BETTER SEX) THROUGH ALCOHOL

DRINK THIN

ANTHONY W. HADDAD

The European Union Declares War on Sweden

A Special Report By Larry Waters

A confidential document from the EU Commission's Health Directorate leaked in April has all of Sweden in an uproar. The document describes banning all flavored tobacco products, including Swedish Snus, in the upcoming EU Tobacco Products Directive (TPD).

"It would mean the end of Swedish snus," said EU Parliamentarian Christofer Fjellner bluntly.

Fjellner's statement was echoed by Patrik Hildingsson, Swedish Match AB Vice President of Group Public Affairs-EU. "This would mean the end of Swedish snus as we know it today. For us, this affects our entire portfolio – a number of flavors that have been used for more than 200 years."

Swedish Match (which is for all practical purposes synonymous with Swedish snus), produces top brands such as General, Ettan, Grov, Göteborgs Rapé, and Catch (among others), leaving SM with an 85% market share in Sweden.

Swedish Citizens Outraged by Secret EU Snus Ban Plan

If the EU Commission themselves leaked the proposed ban on all tobacco flavorings to gauge public response, they seriously underestimated the wrath of Swedish public. Poll numbers are changing constantly, but the most recent we have

of this writing from the Swedish publication *Aftonbladet* is of 86,270 respondents, 76.35% oppose any ban on Swedish snus.

Over one million Swedes use snus; or one in nine Swedish citizens. Not only are Swedish snus users stunned by this development, but Swedes see this as an arrogant targeted betrayal of Sweden by the EU in Brussels.

Sweden originally refused to join the EU because of a politically and scientifically vapid ban the EU had placed on the sale of Swedish snus within the EU. Finally the EU caved to the extent of exempting Sweden itself from the snus ban.

For the last 15+ years, Swedish politicians and their EU representatives have been working for a lifting of the EU snus ban as it unfairly restricts Sweden's right to free trade within the EU. As the new EU TPD is expected to come up for a vote in the 4th quarter of 2012, the stakes and the arguments have risen.

The argument by Sweden to remove the EU snus ban from the TPD was set on its side by this latest development of banning tobacco flavorings. Effectively, the EU is breaking it's original agreement with Sweden by not actually banning snus, but banning all the flavoring ingredients required to produce snus. These flavoring ingredients, like Swedish snus itself, have been regulated as food products since 1970 by the Swedish National Food Administration (Sweden's version of FDA).

This latest action to poison the new TPD, which

Modern Swedes are generally non-confrontational. While the lifting of the current EU Snus Ban would be desirable economically and to promote the public health, many Swedes didn't rush to arms so long as Sweden was still allowed to produce their favorite snuses and sell them within Sweden.

This all changed with the leaked EU Commission Health Directorate proposal. In Europe, #snusriot and #snus were the top trending hashtags on twitter this morning. Anger over the EU betrayal spills beyond snus as tweet after tweet calls for Sweden to secede from the EU and questions what value the EU really is to Sweden.

The original vote in Sweden to join the EU was approved by a very small majority. Millions of Swedes are now wondering if it isn't time to revisit that decision or, at a minimum, re-evaluate what the EU can do *for* Sweden instead of what it can do *to* Sweden.

will be effective for at least 10 to 20 years if history is any guide, reeks of a long standing anti-Swedish bias by the EU central government, if not most of the member nations themselves.

As the Euro crisis continues to threaten the economic implosion of Europe, don't be fooled into thinking the EU is acting only for the sake of the public health any more than FDA is here in the United States. In the end this all boils down to money and power.

While cigarettes are still smoked globally and Big Pharmaceutical's ineffective and even dangerous products like Chantix are praised by the anti-nicotine extremists, any form of smokeless or reduced risk tobacco products are hamstrung by bureaucratic hurdle after hurdle. Anti-all-tobacco junk science is quoted as gospel while real science and the living laboratory which is Sweden ignored and buried by most of the mainstream media; ignored by the Anti-Snus Extremists, whether in Europe or North America.

Swedish politicians, appointed officials, and representatives to the EU have loudly joined the Swedish masses vowing this measure will not pass. Previously lukewarm politicos are now standing on the barricades vowing to protect snus and snus ingredients from EU tampering within Sweden.

Instead of retreating, EU spokesmen, while explaining that the flavoring bans were focused on cigarettes, agreed they "probably could affect" other tobacco products including Swedish snus and presumably nasal snuff produced and sold, often untaxed, in other EU countries. Predictably, the fires of Swedish outrage were fanned even higher.

I began to wonder what the EU Commission was really trying to accomplish with the unexplained "leaking" of the Tobacco Flavoring Ban proposal and their apparent defense of it.

"Hey Sweden, we even made our flag yellow and blue just like yours. Can we hang out now?" asks a smitten European Union.

So why was EU plan leaked in the first place and what is the real purpose for it?

I began to wonder what the EU Commission was really trying to accomplish with the unexplained "leaking" of the Tobacco Flavoring Ban proposal and their apparent defense of it. In sifting through numerous Swedish and European press reports and political pronouncements concerning the Snus Flavoring Ban, I discovered a statement which was glaringly different than most others-especially the remarks of most Swedish politicians.

It came from the Swedish Food Workers Union which represents snus industry workers. They had sent an open letter to Swedish Health Minister Maria Larsson demanding action on lifting the Swedish snus ban in the EU. "Sweden has a unique ability with Swedish snus to improve the European public health while Swedish exports will be strengthened."

I reviewed Larsson's comments concerning the snus ingredients ban and like other Government officials, she was strident in her opposition to the snus flavoring ban. In an interview with *Aftonbladet*, she stated ""We will not give in, but will actively promote that the Swedish exception (concerning snus) should be maintained." She has previously been mum on the subject of lifting the overall EU snus ban already in place.

EU Commission spokesman on health issues, Frédéric Vincent, said that the Commission's position with respect to snus is unchanged--that

Sweden has an exemption from the current snus the ban in the EU. He also reiterated that it is unlikely that the Commission will table a proposal that this ban on snus in the rest of the EU be lifted. In short, Larsson and the vast majority of Swedish officials are prepared to go down fighting for the freedom of snus users in their country.

Vincent, speaking for the EU Health Commission, gave a very vague reassurance but conversely was very specific in stating that the lifting of the EU Snus ban was simply not going to happen.

The EU Commission is engaged in political theater and Sweden, at least at this point, is following the EU's script to the letter. In the end, the snus ingredients ban will be defeated. Sweden won't pull out of the EU. Swedish politicos will hold their swords high and trumpet Sweden's victory over Brussels loudly and often.

Their price for this "victory" will be a new EU Tobacco Products Directive which will continue the current EU Snus Ban for decades to come. Then the political curtain will fall, leaving Sweden no better off than it was before. The EU Commission will be the ones on stage bowing to the loud applause from detractors of all things Swedish (including tobacco)- unless Sweden takes their newfound boldness and rewrites the ending to the TPD saga before time runs out.

Even before they were married, Bela had taught fifth (and final) wife Hope how to properly clean, pack and light his pipe. Shades of Curt Jurgens! (See our first issue)

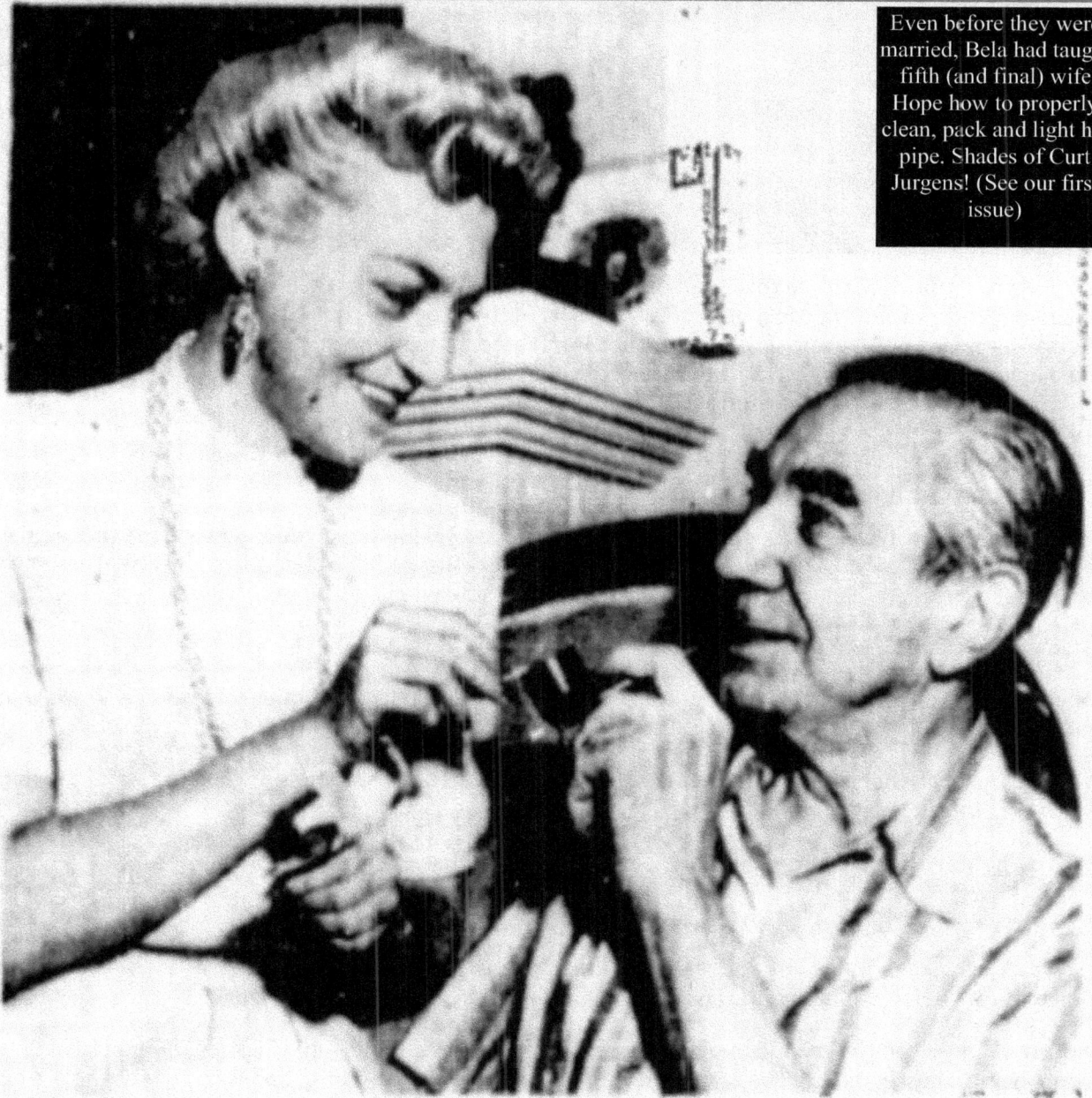

CUPID TAGS HORROR ACTOR LUGOSI

Hollywood, Calif., Aug. 24 — The girl who wrote him encouraging letters while he was taking the cure for the drug habit is the choice of a wife for horror actor Bela Lugosi, shown here with the girl he will wed tonight — Hope Lininger, 40, a movie studio cutting - room clerk. A copyright story in a Los Angeles newspaper said the romance was born when Miss Lininger wrote Lugosi daily anonymous letters while he was taking an addiction cure in a state hospital. Lugosi was released this month and found the note writer after a search. — AP Wirephoto.

The Most Expensive Snuff in the World

A Special Fang-in-Cheek Ephemeris Travelogue by

Beck Linden

"You've pretty much *got* to do this," came the voice on the other end of the line. It was Micah Rimel, the Managing Editor of the sTe. He'd been after me for months to do an article about the snuff in some of the strange countries I've been to. Problem is, once I get there, I usually spend a lot of time getting drunk and partying, and I forget to ask the locals about snuff.

"The next issue's going to be about vampires and Bela Lugosi and Transylvania and blah blah blah" he went on. I don't care. The last sexy vampire I saw was Julian Sands in *Tale of a Vampire*. Now I hear that they sparkle. Meh.

I was going to be traveling through the former Soviet Block, taking pictures for a magazine that actually pays their contributors. At one point in the journey, I was going to have to go through the Carpathian mountains by train. When Micah heard this, he basically stalked me until I said "yes."

"Give me the details," I huffed.

"There's a type of snuff that's made out there that we got our hands on a couple of years back. We want you to find the company that manufactured it."

"Why not just call them, or e-mail them?" After all, this is 2012. Five seconds of googling should turn up everything they need.

"Well..." he started. "It's a little bit more complicated than that. Have you got a minute?"

****

Two years ago a man walks into the office of *The Ephemeris.* He's pale, he's shaking; he looks like a drug addict. Micah, being the humanitarian that he is, offers the guy a sandwich.

The guy collapses on the ground, muttering something about "der blut" and "ist der schnupftabak". Micah, being a descendant of Erwin Rommel, understood the word "tabak" and figured that the old man wanted free samples or something. "We don't have much around here," Micah explained. "They don't send us any samples because the FDA doesn't allow it and all of the smokeless tobacco manufacturers that we write about in our magazine comply fully to the letter of the law regarding handing out free samples. But I have some coupons for Marlboro cigarettes here in my desk somewhere. The Philip Morris coupons are legal, because Obama smokes them."

But the man was persistent. "Der schnupftabak!" he screamed.

Micah was now reaching for his Bowie knife that he keeps hidden under his typewriter. The man bolted from the floor one last time, and threw something shiny on Micah's desk. The man fell back on the ground, lifeless.

A Journey to Carpathian Ruthenia in search of Uskat Krüt

"Oh, snap!" Micah said, reaching for the phone. He dialed 911 and got in touch with an operator. "There's a crazy guy that just ran in my office wanting tobacco! Now he's having some kind of stroke or something, please send an ambulance!"

The dispassionate voice on the other end inquired as to what the man was wearing. "Shit, I don't know," Micah replied. "Bum clothes? Homeless garb? Let me check." He leaned over the desk cautiously, only to find a faded pair of rubber boots. The man had vanished completely. "Uh, get this," he said. "Dude's gone. But he left his boots. And a pile of dirt. Sarah just vacuumed in here, so she's going to be pissed!"

The police arrived shortly thereafter and inspected the pile of soot and Micah's pupils in an effort to determine what was actually going on. "Are you sure you're not on those bath salts that I've been hearing about?" asked an incredulous Captain Jim McClusky. "Are you a salter?"

No stranger to police harassment, Micah avoided the allegations. "I've never done drugs in my life. I'm not high. I don't hallucinate." Which was the God's honest truth. "This guy came in all weird and then vanished, leaving a pile of dirty ashes that my hausfrau is going to have to clean up first thing in the morning, if she knows what's good for her."

The cops left, leaving Micah with a pair of boots and a pile of ashes. He picked up the phone to call his publisher, Rob Hubbard. Waiting for Rob to pick up the phone, Micah noticed the silver amulet laying on the desk. He had forgotten that the homeless guy tossed it at him right before vanishing. He picked it up and held it in his hand just as Rob's voicemail kicked on. Micah waited for Rob's customary greeting to play ("*Check's in the mail!*") before the beep. He left a brief message retelling the day's events, then placed the amulet in the drawer and went on to spend the night at Fumée, the local brothel.

The next day, Editor-n-Chief Mick Hellwig and ailing President Rob Hubbard were sitting in the office of *The Ephemeris*, looking at the strange amulet and listening to Micah's bizarre story. Rob picked up the lidded silver curio and twisted the top off. "Grab that bowl," he muttered to Mick. Rob turned the amulet upside down and emptied its contents.

"Looks like snuff," Mick said.

"Looks like Paprika," Rob offered.

"Let's snort it!" Micah exclaimed.

They each took turns passing the bowl around and taking a pinch. "Well, here's to nothing," Mick said, and they all took a heaping sniff into each nostril.

As soon as the snuff entered their nasal passages and found its way into their bloodstream, they were knocked to the ground. Literally. "It was like an invisible Mike Tyson punched me in the nose and knocked me back about four feet," Rob explained to me later. "And it really hurt, because I have a big French nose." The other guys were similarly winded. "Hell, I'm as big as Mike Tyson," Mick said, "So it was kind of like getting hit by a drunk on a snowplow."

What followed next was a dazed, semi-hallucinatory euphoria. The three men laid on the carpet, not saying anything. "I had the nicotine buzz of a lifetime," recalled Micah. "I was hearing colors and seeing sounds."

Mick described it somewhat differently. "I felt at peace for the first time in my life. Like angels had put me on a bed made of fluffy pillows and told me that everything was going to be OK. I also noticed quite a bit of tonka bean in the recipe."

Rob recalled it being more of an aniseed flavor. "There was something you couldn't quite put your finger on. But it felt like there was a party in my brain and everyone was invited."

After the bliss trip had ended, the guys decided to call in an expert. "Simon knows more about snuff and snuffboxes than anyone else in this country," Mick said, referring to *The Ephemeris's* resident snuff collector Simon Handelsman. "I kept trying to take a picture on my phone to email him, but it just wouldn't work. And it wouldn't work on any of the other cameras we used, either. Everything just came out too dark or too blurry."

"Let's just drive out to his place and show him the damn thing," Micah offered. The three piled into Micah's '87 Sentra and headed towards Massachusetts. After a couple of hours, Mick had to stop and pee, so they pulled over at a rest stop. What happened next threw everyone for a loop.

"I pulled out the amulet-snuffbox thing," Rob said, "and it was melting. It had turned into a formless gob of silver. And it burned the crap out of me at its touch. I threw it on the floorboard and it melted through that and into the pavement underneath. It sizzled, like cooking oil, and then it was gone for good."

The three men drove back to the office and began sketching a picture of the amulet. They faxed it over to Simon, who called them immediately and asked them where they got it. After explaining the disappearing hobo story for the seventeenth time, Micah handed the phone back to Mick. Mick grumbled into the line and hung up.

"So what's the story, morning glory?" Rob asked Mick.

"Uh, better sit down for this one," he said.

****

According to Simon, the amulet/snuffbox/silver trinket was at least 400 years old, manufactured in what is present day Romania. There were only two known to still exist, with the other belonging to a private collector in Austria. They were made by unknown craftsmen, and legend had it that the nails that were used during Christ's crucifixion were smelted down into the silver to give its user protection against evil.

"What kind of evil?" Micah asked.

"I don't know," Simon replied. "Witchcraft, werewolves, vampires, boogeymen... whatever folk superstitions were native to that area."

"Why would it melt in the sunlight?" Rob asked.

"Who knows?" Simon answered. "Maybe it was a counterfeit. Maybe it had a chemical reaction to something around it. You did mention that it was being waved around by a crazy homeless guy, right?"

Micah thought back to the creepy stranger. "Yeah, maybe he could have had leprosy or something."

"But what about the snuff?" Mick asked. "It was definitely some sort of tobacco, but I've never had anything strong enough to literally knock me on my ass."

The sound of paper shuffling on Simon's end filled the speakerphone. "I have one lead. Granted, it's a very minor lead, and it may have nothing to do with your snuff chalice or the snuff itself. But around the same time that the amulets were forged, there was a snuff mill in that village that the locals claimed was cursed. One by one, the inhabitants of the town left the village until only the snuff mill remained. The trees and shrubbery grew up so high that the mill became completely covered and after a couple of hundred years, the entire area was one big dense jungle. But I have no record of the mill having ever been closed. Maybe the ruins are still there?"

"Where is this village?" Micah asked.

"You won't find it on any map, that's for sure. I don't have the exact coordinates, but I made a transparent copy of a 17th century map and placed it over a modern map of the same area, and I think there's a chance that it's buried in the woods of Carpathian Rumenia."

"Where the hell is Carpathian Rumenia?" Mick asked.

"Is that the same thing as the Trans-Carpathian Mountains?" Rob said.

"Yes," replied Simon. "The region stretches all throughout Eastern Europe, from Czechoslovakia and Poland, down through Hungary and the Ukraine, all the way down to Romania and Serbia."

"So, how long does it take to get through there?" Micah asked.

"Uh..." Simon said. "The entire range is over a thousand miles long."

"Son of a whore!" Micah exclaimed. "You mean that there may be the ruins of an ancient snuff mill buried in the middle of an 1100 mile mountain range that may or may not shed some light on this magical disappearing knockout snuff that a hobo threw at me?"

"Easy..." Simon replied cooly. "I've got it narrowed down to the Eastern Carpathians. The area was once part of Poland, Austria and Hungary but it's pretty much Romanian and Serbian territory now."

"Well, how are we supposed to find it?" Rob asked.

"If it were me," Simon answered, "And it wouldn't be me, because I don't really care enough to investigate this any further..." Rob, Mick and Micah simultaneously rolled their eyes. It was impossible to tear Simon away from his antique snuffbox store. "... But I would probably start in Bucharest and work my way down to Transylvania, trying to glean as much information from the locals as possible. Somebody has to know the location, since this chalice is, or was, still in circulation. The legends in that part of the world never die."

After hanging up with Simon, Micah and Mick asked Rob what type of travel funds *The Ephemeris* had in its reserves. "Well, if one of you needs a bus ticket to Atlanta, I've got you covered. Flying to Romania? Not going to happen."

The three men looked at the ground, feeling somewhat defeated. "Wait a minute..." Micah had that look in his eye. "I know this chick that travels all around the world writing for a leftist hippie magazine in Austin that is all about communist socialism. I'm sure she flies that way all the time!"

CARPATHO-RUSYN HOMELAND

International
boundaries, 1993

Transcarpathian Oblast
(Subcarpathian Rus')

Carpatho-Rusyn settlement,
1910

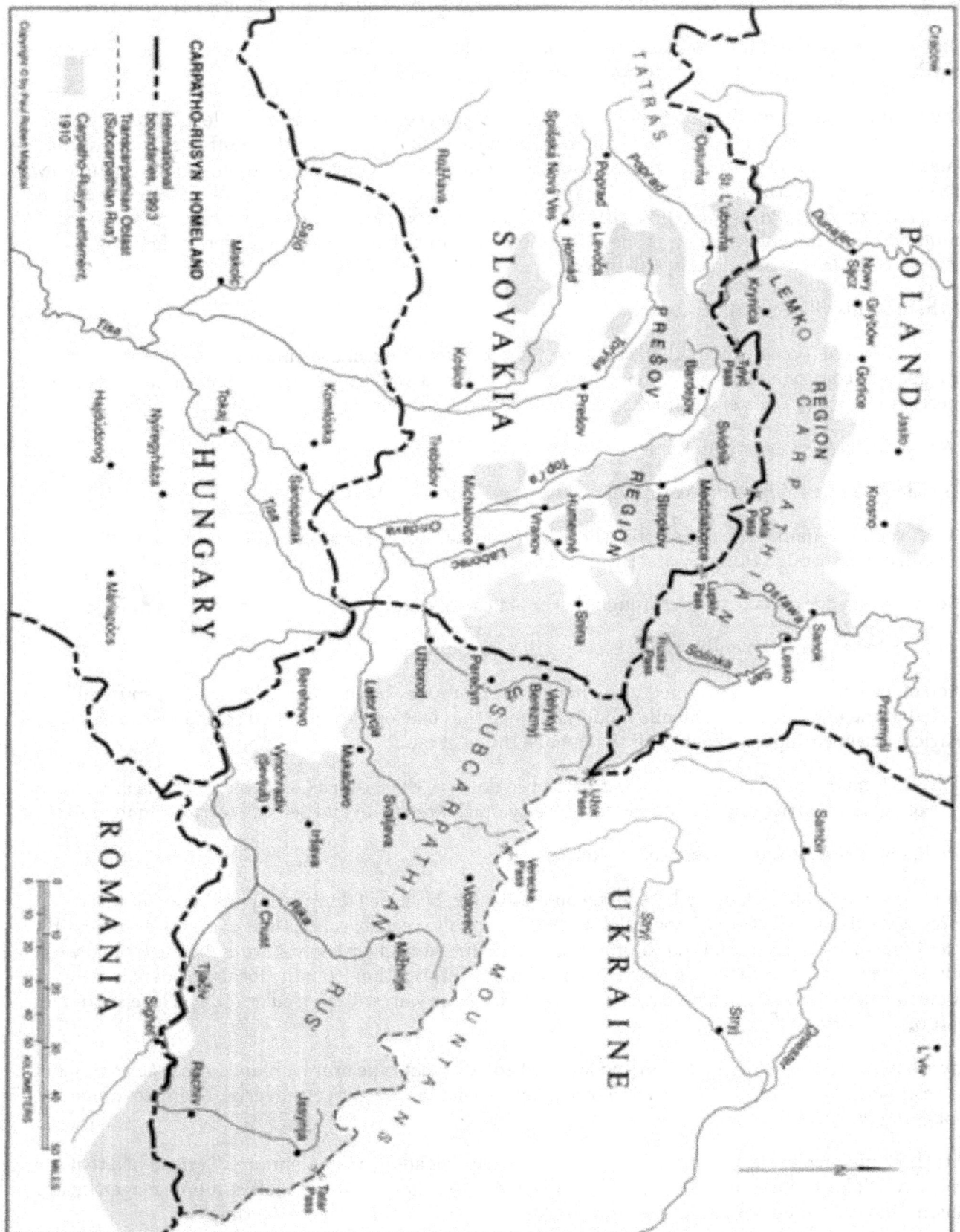

Copyright © by Paul Robert Magocsi

"Give her a call," Mick said. "See if she's going out that way anytime soon and tell her we'll pay her expenses if she investigates this thing for us."

"I'll try," Micah said.

"Is she hot?" Rob inquired.

"Yeah, pretty hot," Micah answered. "Why?"

"Because we only hire hot women to write for *The Ephemeris*. I want to keep it that way."

****

So about a year had gone by between the aforementioned incident and my commission from Micah to find out all that I knew about this mysterious snuff. He had made a contact or two in the area and passed their info on to me. I have to admit, I was a little intrigued by the whole thing. I hoped that I had enough time after the Bela Kun memorial in Hungary to investigate it further.

By rail I traveled to Uzhorod, which is sort of a central location to the Carpathians. It borders the Ukraine and Slovakia and is pretty much the best starting point for investigating the mountain region in which I was to do my research.

I decided, on a whim, to start my tracking (where else?) but Transylvania. It's in the center of the Trans Carpathians, so depending on what leads I picked up, I could easily navigate my way north or south in the correct direction.

Transylvania isn't at all like the vampire movies that play late night, with creepy castles and spooks running wild. It's fairly modern, but touches of the ancient ways still dot the landscape. It was at one such castle, the Porta Praetoria, where I met my first contact, a man who wished to remain nameless.

With great hesitancy I approached the ancient fort and began to ascend its stairs. I had climbed all of ten feet when a man stepped out from the shadows of a column. He was shabbily dressed, with a long beard and eyes so blue that they looked almost inhuman. He was smoking a hand-rolled cigarette. It looked like it was mostly paper and with hardly any tobacco inside.

"So," he said in a thick Slavic accent, "You are the girl that comes to find the elixir."

"No, I'm here to find out about some snuff." He eyed me contemptuously and flicked his cigarette away.

"To you, snuff. In Rus, elixir." With that we descended the stairs and walked about a quarter mile away from the fort. I could hear the sound of running water and knew we were near a river. Eventually we reached a small dock with a canoe tied to one of its posts. The man motioned at me to get inside.

"I'm not getting into that thing with you!"

"Come. It is only way."

"Can't we rent a car or something?" I asked. "Aren't there any roads to drive there? And where exactly *are* we going?"

By the time I had finished my questioning, he had already removed the rope holding the canoe to the dock. "No car. Where we go, no road."

I figured I was making the stupidest mistake of my life, but I climbed in to the boat and set off for the land with no roads.

****

The first hour of the boat ride was fairly pleasant, I must say. Fifty degree temperatures, no mosquitos, no snakes or alligators; it was like a European Everglades that cut through some of the most beautiful mountain scenery this side of the Appalachians.

I noticed that I was out of water, and I dipped my empty bottle into the crystal clear river to refill it. Slavic Man instantly knocked the water bottle out of my hands and said that I must never drink from this part of the Olt.

"Why?" I asked.

"Too much mercury."

"Well, do you have anything to drink in that little cooler box under your seat?"

He eyed me for a second before reaching into the icebox. He pulled out a blue glass bottle with a white rubber cork.

"What is that, wine?"

"No," he said. "Sulphur water. It good for you."

I looked at the cloudy looking liquid and decided that I would rather remain thirsty.

"Everyone in America drink bottle water. Everyone in Romania drink sulphur water."

Well, I thought, *when have I ever turned down a drink before?* I took a big swig and forced it down. Drinking sulphur water is like swallowing a thousand farts. Surprisingly, I didn't puke it back up. I corked the bottle and handed it back to Slavic Man. His eyes danced wildly and his mouth formed a crooked grin. "You like?"

"Don't speak to me."

He paddled the next mile in silence while I gradually began to doze off.

****

When I awoke, it was barely dawn of the next day. I had slept through the late afternoon and all through the night. Slavic Man was tying the canoe to a piece of tree that was jutting out of the surface of the water.

"So...." I yawned. "How many times did you grope me while I was passed out?"

He grunted. "Grope... is like rape? I did not rape you."

"That's good to know."

We climbed out of the canoe and I took in the scenery. We were still on the Olt River, but it had narrowed significantly from the wide expanse we originally paddled down. I couldn't really see anything past a bend in the water about a quarter mile down.

"Why are we stopping here, exactly?" I asked.

"This is end of line for me. I shall take you no further."

"Well, where the hell am I?"

"You are very near the village of Balánbánya. There you shall find what you are looking for. Follow the wood around the bend and go past the old copper mines. They will find you."

"They who?" I asked.

"You will see," he answered, without a hint of a smile one his face. "Good luck. Don't get graped."

He paddled off into the opposite direction and I began to make my way down the riverbank that as I had been instructed. The water seemed more clear here, drinkable even. I cupped as much of it as I could in my hands and spat the nastiness of the previous day out of my mouth. Then I drank about a pint of the coolest, sweetest water I had ever tasted. It reminded me of the old Crystal Light commercials, where the woman looked as though she was so parched that if she stopped drinking the diet lemonade, she would shrivel up and die.

I wandered through the forest and took note of the ancient trees. One thing I've noticed in my travels is that the woods in any one place are unique; the Pine Barrens of New Jersey have nothing in common with the foothills of North Carolina for instance. The Black Forest of Germany resembles nothing on earth, even other Bavarian forests. So it was with the land of Balánbánya, whose shrubbery and foliage looked as though it concealed mythological horrors that Westerners have never even heard of. There was no sound whatsoever. No birds flying, no insects chirping; just dead silence. I felt like I was wearing earplugs.

As I crossed the bend in the river, I noticed a waterfall in the distance. The terrain had turned from woodsy to rocky, and I had to carefully balance myself on the jutting boulders to avoid slipping into the river, which was becoming more shallow as I went along. Eventually I reached the waterfall, which looked like something out of one of those pamphlets they give you at state parks to entice you into spending $45 a night to camp there. Something about the crystal clear water cascading down the rocks was almost hypnotic, like watching a bonfire climb higher and higher.

Having not bathed in a couple of days, I decided that I would step under the waterfall and catch a quick shower. Not having any soap didn't bother me, I just needed to feel that luxurious stream on my skin. I took off my shorts and t-shirt that were glued to my body and undid my Converse sneakers. (I don't wear panties or bras, just in case you're wondering why I didn't mention them.) I stood under the waterfall for what felt like hours, just letting the water rinse away the grime and dirt off my skin.

As the water rolled through my hair and flowed between my breasts, I opened my eyes and nearly fainted. There was a woman, perched on the rock in front of me, glaring at me intently. My hands scrambled to cover my exposed parts. The girl still stared. For about twenty seconds we stood there awkwardly looking at each other in silence. She never blinked. Her long black dress billowed slightly in the breeze.

She finally broke the silence. "Are you the American?" she asked, in a heavy Hungarian accent.

"Uh... yeah. I guess. Could you hand me those clothes next to you?"

She reached over without taking her eyes off of me and retrieved my clothing. Her pupils locked on mine, she sniffed my shorts and licked her lips. Tossing them my way, I hurriedly dressed and walked out from under the waterfall.

"I am Greta. The others are waiting."

"Well," I said. "Let's not procrastinate. The whole time I was in the boat, I kept saying 'paddle faster, the others are waiting' because I know just how important these people are; you know, these Others whom I know nothing absolutely nothing about." Either she didn't understand American sarcasm or she just didn't care, since her face remained the same chiseled statue it had been since I caught her peeping at me in the waterfall.

We walked down the narrow pathway that led to the riverbank. At first, I could see nothing. Greta pointed up a hill a few meters away and touched my shoulder. I waited for her to say something, like *the people you're looking for are up there,* or even *get your ass up that hill,* but nada. She just stared up at the direction she was pointing me towards.

With a great deal of difficulty, I made my way up the steep hill, bruising my knees and scratching my arms in the process. The hill didn't look that tall from the ground, but it seemed to gain twenty feet for every six inches I managed. After about ten minutes, I sat down to rest. I looked down at the river where I last saw Greta, but she was gone. I figured she must have had some other naked women to go look at.

I finally reached the top of the hill. I pulled myself up and was surprised to see that the flat land I had envisioned was instead marred with more craggy boulders. I cussed under my breath and sat down. I was really sick of rocks. Sick of water. Sick of foreign... *stuff.* If this was America, there would be a Starbucks at the top of the hill instead of a bunch of granite. But this was Romania. Hell, I wondered if there was even a McDonald's anywhere in the entire country.

I heard what sounded like giggling coming from atop one of the closer boulders. I followed the sound until I came across two women, laying on a rock. They were sunning themselves like rattlesnakes. The two girls, one with black hair and the other kind of a reddish brown, didn't seem to notice me. They were both looking into each other's eyes, whispering in a language I didn't understand.

The black haired girl abruptly looked up at me. "Welcome," was all she said. The redhead started giggling some more.

"Are you 'the others' I keep hearing about?" I asked, not impolitely.

They started giggling again. "We are many things to many people," answered the brunette. *I bet you are,* I thought to myself. *Right now you look like a couple of Czech prostitutes that just earned your nightly keep.*

Both girls laughed loudly. They were now glaring at me, with a look of pure hatred. The redhead spoke. "We are many things, this is true... but we are not whores."

"Oh shit," I said. "But you *are* telepathic?" They both nodded. This was starting to get interesting.

"We're also vampires," the black haired girl said. "In case you haven't figured that out yet."

Before I could say anything else, the redhead reached under the rock and pulled out a dark red snake, at least four feet long and the diameter of a Coke can. With a flick of her wrist, she broke the serpent's neck and handed the now-dead snake to the black haired girl.

Blackie and Red both opened their mouths. Their canine teeth grew about three quarters of an inch longer. They simultaneously bit down on the snake and sucked the blood out of its rubbery corpse. They moaned as they sucked, deriving an almost sexual ecstasy from the act. The entire scene went on for about two minutes. At the end, the snake's dark red blood covered their faces and what little clothing they were wearing. Blackie flung the shriveled snake down on the ground. It was now only about the width of a penny.

"I am Lillith," the black haired girl said. She pointed at the redhead. "She is nameless." The redhead nodded in agreement. "We must now bathe." She pointed at the river, and we made our way down the hill.

"So who was the other girl?" I asked. "The one who led me to you?"

Lillith looked at me. Her accent, while not quite as thick as Greta's, was still quite pronounced. "Greta is my slave. She does what I ask and nothing more."

"So... is this some sort of a Bondage or S&M type thing?" I innocently questioned.

"Greta gives me no reason to punish her," Lillith answered. "I do not bind her with anything. She comes to me willingly. If you mean to ask if we are sexual together, then yes, we are. I am sexual with many people." The nameless girl looked over fondly at Lillith, perhaps remembering a recent tryst the two had together.

We got to the riverbank and the girls crept in until the water was about chest high. "So, do you make this snuff or not?" I asked, as they rinsed the blood from their mouths. Neither answered.

"Do you know why we bathe in the Olt River?" Lillith asked me. "No," I answered. "Do you not have any running water or electricity in this town?" Again, nada response to the sarcasm.

"We bathe here because this is where Vlad Tepesh was baptized," Lillith answered. "So was Bela Lugosi," the nameless redhead muttered.

"You never answered my question about the snuff."

Lillith looked up at me with a quizzical look in her eyes. "We know that this is all you care about, but you are being quite rude in insisting we tell you our secrets post-haste. Your answers will come in time."

"I'm not *trying* to be rude," I replied. "Three dorks that publish a snuff magazine knew a guy who knew a guy who knew a guy that said that there was some secret snuff company buried deep in these woods. I meet this big, burly stinky man who has me drink fart water. Then I try to take a shower and Lisbeth Salander's staring at me sniffing my panties. Then I climb a hill and you two pop fangs and suck off a snake and read my mind and did I mention that I'm not getting paid anything for this excursion?"

Lillith turned her back to me and continued bathing. At times, her and the nameless one would take turns cleaning each other's bodies. It was like a late-night Cinemax softcore porn movie. The only thing missing was the slow-motion closeups and soft-focus lens. But I have to admit, I was getting a little turned on either way.

"You may join us if you wish," Lillith said, almost cooing.

"No thanks," I said. "I'll wait till I find a hotel with hot water and soap."

"As you wish," Lillith replied. They finished their water lily routine and climbed out of the water.

"Where is your snuff mill? Or office, or whatever the hell it is I'm supposed to get pictures of?"

Lillith pointed at the mouth of the waterfall. "Where you were bathing; that is the entrance." I looked at her like she was crazy, but then I realized that everything I had witnessed this day was unbelievable.

"So it's like a James Bond movie? Blofield's secret headquarters are behind the rocks or something?"

Lillith smiled. "Something like that." We walked towards the waterfall, which was flanked on both sides by brick walls scattered with foreign graffiti. "So," I asked her, "If you two are real vampires, then how come you're out here in the daylight, not burning?"

"There is the vampire," she said, "then there is the vampire legend. We are nocturnal creatures, it's true, but we are not allergic to sunlight. Or garlic. Or a crucifix. Our immune systems are more resilient than yours, so we can survive things like gunshots or stab wounds that would probably kill someone like you. Otherwise, we are the same as humans. Except for our diets."

We walked through the waterfall and into a cavern that was pitch black. "Oh," Lillith said, "we can also see in the dark, so take my hand." We went about forty or fifty paces and the nameless one opened a wooden door framed into the cave wall. It opened into another section of forest. The daylight pierced my eyes after the stint in the pitch black cave. I could barely make out the skeletal figure of an abandoned building. Giant stone walls that looked like a cross between a gristmill and a castle towered over the landscape.

"These ruins... this is where you work?" I asked. Neither one answered as we made our way towards the building. There was a narrow footpath that lead toward one of the entrances to the structure. The nameless one ducked under the short doorway and I followed.

Lillith approached a six foot tall boulder that looked like it may have weighed two tons. Amazingly, she pushed it away with barely any effort. "Oh, we also have super strength," she added, as if I wasn't paying attention. The boulder concealed an entranceway that led under the building.

The tunnel was surprisingly modern; concrete walls, carpeted flooring and humming fluorescent lights gave it the air of a typical business office. "Nice digs," I said. Lillith let out a sharp whistle and the boulder behind us rolled back into place. Suddenly Greta appeared in front of us, her hands clasped together as if in prayer. "Welcome back, my mistress," she greeted Lillith.

With a wave of her hand, Lillith dismissed Greta and she silently retreated down an opposite hall. The nameless one walked ahead of us and opened a door to the right and entered. I heard the click-clack of her heels on porcelain tile and the buzz of an exhaust fan as she flicked the light switch on. "She pees quite often," Lillith said. "You may also use that room once she is finished. Or while she is in there, if you prefer."

"I'll wait," I said. "So what is this place? Is this like your corporate headquarters or is this where you make the snuff?"

"You shall soon see," Lillith said, putting her arm around my shoulder. "We have many things to show you..." STE

Check out our next issue for the conclusion to this quirky trip through vampire land!

The Snuff Box

By Simon Handelsman

SHAPING UP TO SNUFF

In the last issue, we reviewed some wooden snuff boxes that were carved into animal shapes. However, many more wooden snuffs were carved into the forms of things. Some are impractical to carry in the pockets and must have been meant for the desk or workshop table. But, all had an appeal to the snuff box buyer, who had many choices from a multitude of round and rectangular boxes. Their unique shapes gave them a special quality for the original buyer and thus, a special place in our collections of snuff boxes.

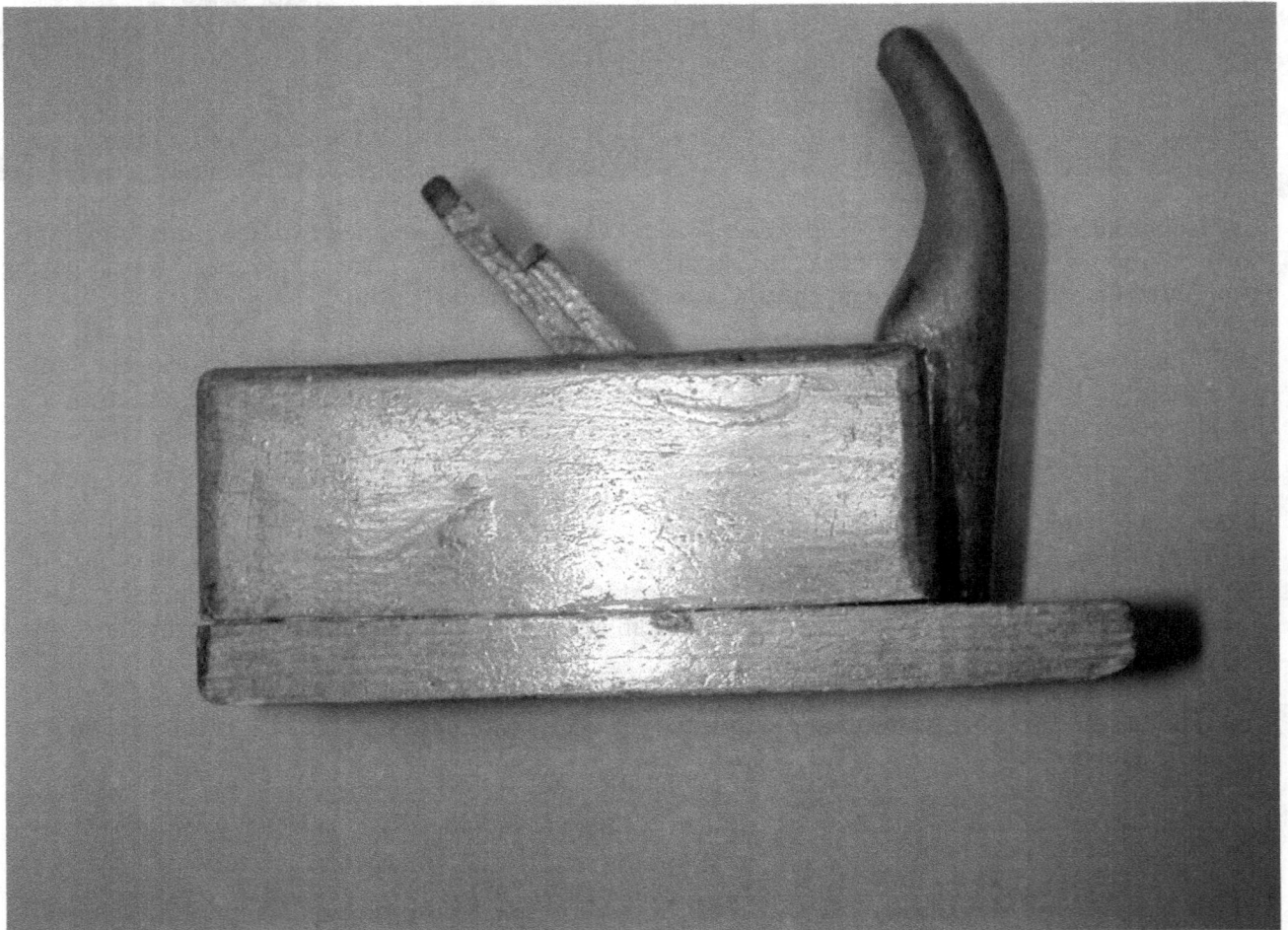

The snuff box on the preceding page is made in the shape of wood smoothing planes. Woodworkers have always been snuffers...too much tinder around to be lighting cigars, pipes and cigarettes; plus working with hot ashes sticking out of your mouth can be dangerous. The more flammable the environment, the greater the chance that snuff will be the preferred choice for tobacco use.

Most of these plane boxes are very well constructed and perhaps were made by the woodworkers themselves. The smoothing plane box requires the vertical handle in front to be slid upward out of its mortise to allow the horizontal lid to slide forward to reach the interior. The box is well used and has some repairs.

This barrel snuff is shaped like a hogshead, which was an early shipping container for tobacco. This is not a common shape, considering how suitable it seems for a snuff box. The example above has a lid at one end and raised ridges to represent the metal hoops. The staves are indicated by lines drawn in ink.

In Colonial Virginia, tobacco was used as currency. The value of this cash crop to the early settlers caused more planting and less concern about quality. Planters were sending stems and dirt packed in with the tobacco leaf. In 1730, a law was passed to protect quality and quantity. All tobacco was packed in hogshead barrels, about 1000 pounds, and shipped to central inspection stations to be examined before being shipped to England. If there was a bumper crop, tobacco was destroyed to support the market price.

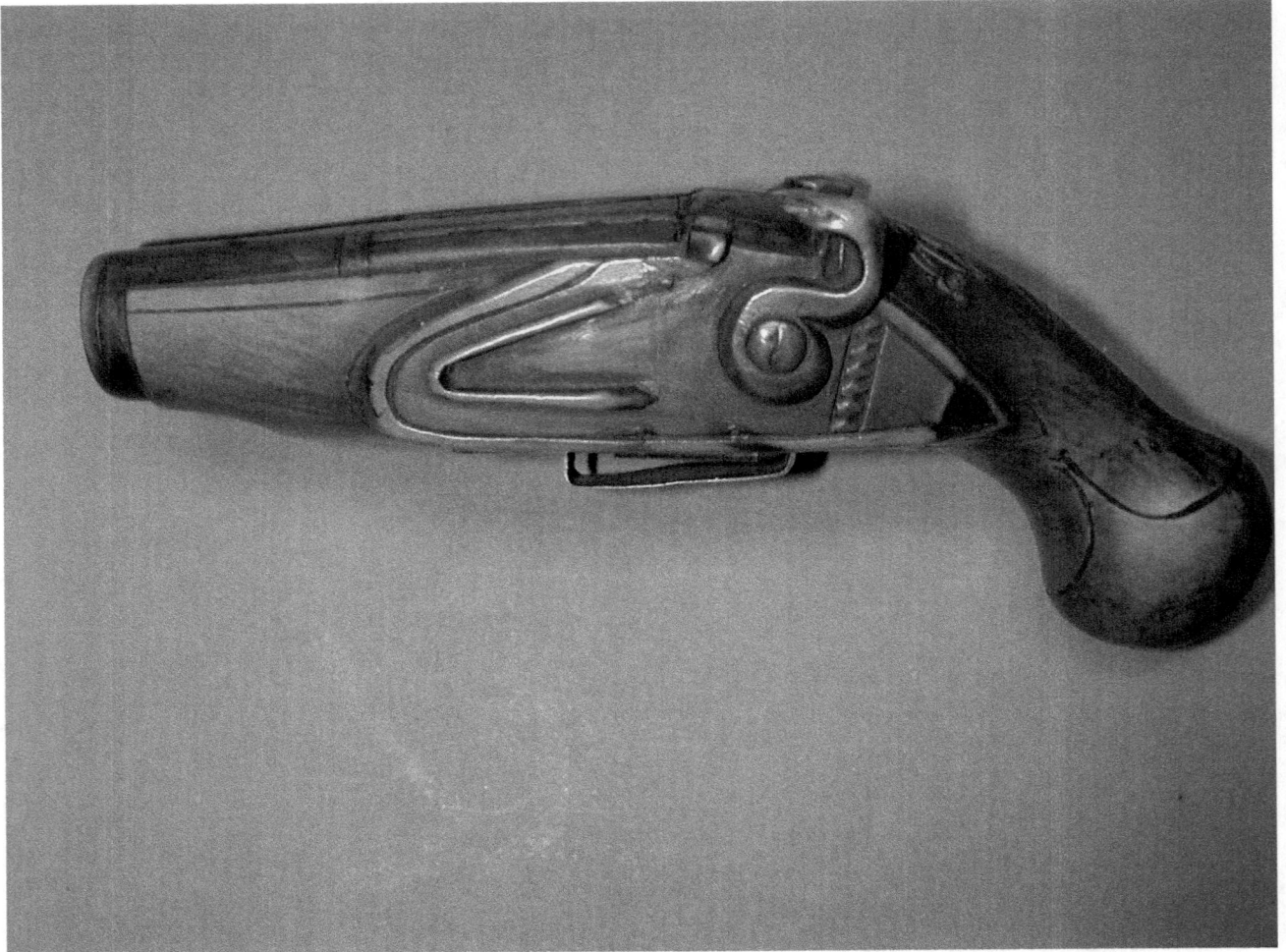

Most pistol shaped snuff boxes show a gun with two barrels side by side. While this is a common configuration for a shot gun, it is unusual for a pistol. Perhaps, a single barrel layout was thought to be too narrow to allow a cavity large enough for snuff. Any opening in a snuff box should be large enough to insert two fingers or small enough to act as a spout to pour out the powder. Regardless, most of the pistol snuffs encountered are two barreled.

This gun is a good representation of an actual two barreled pistol made in the mid 18th century. Since a muzzleloading barrel only allowed one shot, multi-barrels were popular. The firing mechanism is flintlock. Parts of the mechanism have been stylized or are missing, but the incised detail on the barrels and the carvings on the wrist are accurate to a real gun. The lid is in the bottom of the gun with a brass loop which may have suggested a trigger guard or may have been used to hold a strap, allowing the box to be worn.

Book-shaped snuff boxes have obvious appeal to bibliophiles. While they are not rare, a good example is more uncommon than expected. The example above right is exceptional in that it has silver inlays on all six sides. The covers each have a centered inlay with one serving as a sliding lid. The spine has three more inlays with carved ribbing to emulate an old hubbed leather binding. Each of the silver insets have delicate floral engraving. The wood is walnut.

Below: This ship snuffbox is a full 8 inches long and likely a prisoner of war model made by a French prisoner during the Napoleonic wars. The French captives made the best of the POW objects they had around because their army was recruited from all the citizens of France and included many skilled artisans versus the many European armies who conscripted, press ganged and emptied prisons to obtain their soldiers. The snuff box is elegantly shaped with a deep thin keel. The cannon ports are fanciful and made from inlays of dark horn separated by mother of pearl. Long horizontal inlays divide the top and bottom rows.

The cover pivots from the stern to allow the entire deck to move backwards and reveal a full length cavity.

This lid is decoratively inlayed with two rectangles indicating deck cabins and a large four leaf clover, all made from mother of pearl.

We have written before about shoe snuff boxes made from paper maché, but wooden shoes have superior carved detail as compared to the molded forms made from layers of paper and glue. Shoe snuffboxes are more common, as they are a token of love and were given by both sexes.

The example below has an accurate, crossover flap with three button fasteners. The stitching detail is represented by inlayed brass strips and the sole picked out with brass tacks. The lid is hinged at the top, but the rest of the shoes is carved from a single piece of wood.

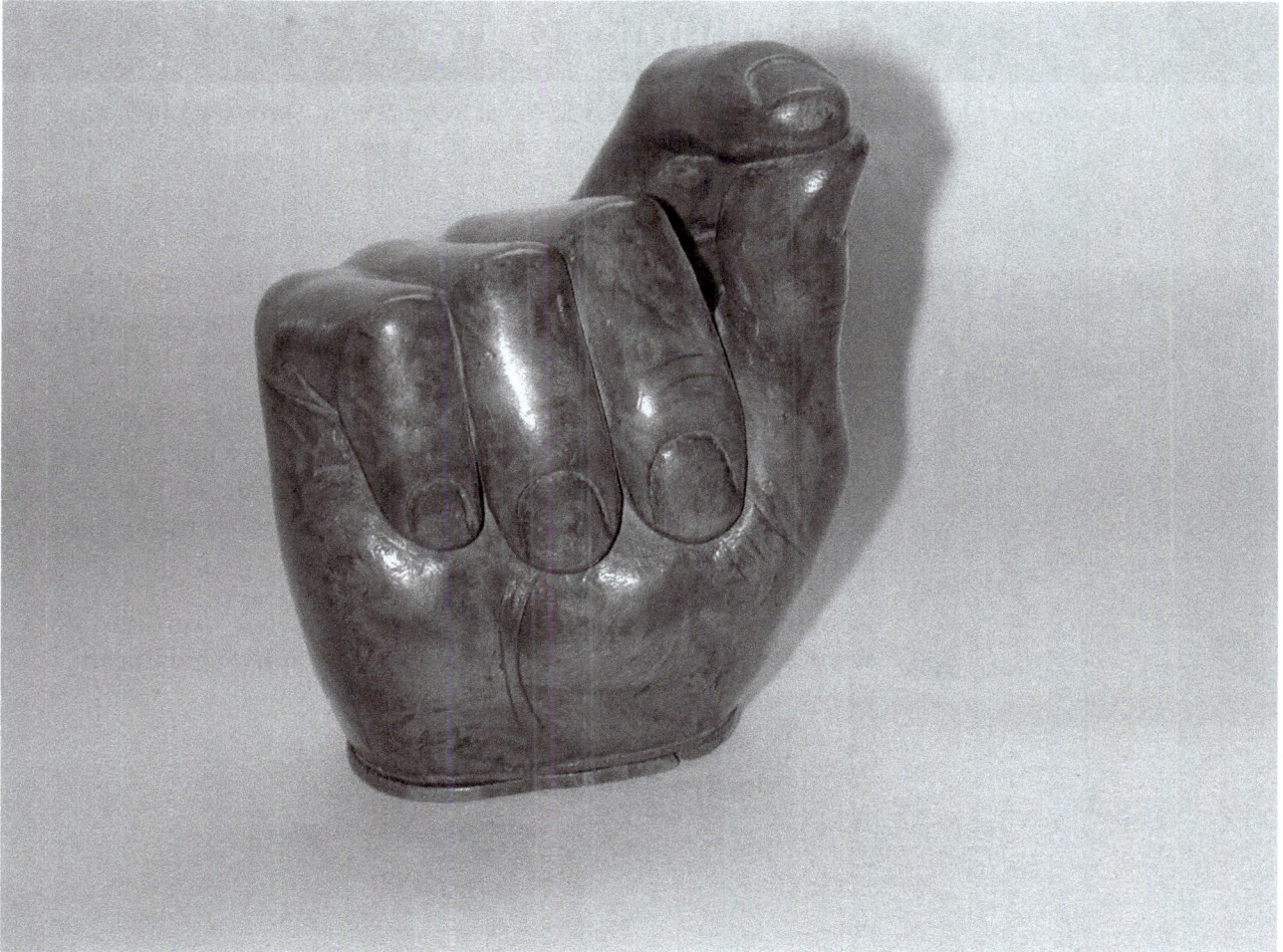

This is a large box carved from a single piece of burl. A wooden burl is very dense with the grain running in all directions and very difficult to carve. The shape is a realistic but simplistic representation of a hand. The creases of the fingers are shown as shallow lines lightly cut into the wood. The lid is in the wrist with the hinge lugs cut into the same piece of wood. The moveable lid is fashioned flat from a decorative burl slice. The box seems made to stand upright.

****

There are no limits to the shapes into which snuff boxes have been carved into and no way to show them all. Our purpose here is not encyclopedic, but more like a docent in a good museum showing some of the popular forms and some of what appeals to the author.

STE

Contributor's Corner

You may have noticed a slew of new names in this month's issue, so we're here to introduce you to them all. We hope you'll enjoy their work as much as we have!

Elisha Cozine

Elisha is the talented lady behind the "Skinny Girl" shoot that will accompany the next several *Winifred Skinny* stories penned exclusively for *The Ephemeris* by noted vagrant Micah D. Rimel.

Mrs. Cozine is a professional photographer with a love of editorial photography. She enjoys coming up with creative concepts for new shoots and sharing with others the art that she creates. She is always happy to be out shooting, no matter the subject.

Booking inquiries can be sent through her website at **www.elishac.webs.com** or to **elishacphotography@gmail.com**.

Jordyn Ballentine

Jordyn is the stunning beauty that adorns the pages of our ongoing series of *Winifred Skinny* western snuff tales penned by suspected arsonist Micah D. Rimel.

The 27 year old Ms. Ballentine, originally from Seattle, now resides in Fayetteville, NC and spends most of her spare time rescuing stray dogs from shelters and off the street.

A talented actress, she has appeared on stage and television since she was 15 and attended the American Academy of Dramatic Arts while living in Los Angeles. Jordyn appears regularly in *The Sleepy Hollow Masquerade* in Raleigh, which will be running into the Halloween season.

For booking information, contact her through her MM page at: **http://www.modelmayhem.com/2766105**

Contributor's Corner

Lillia Luster

Lillia Luster is a professional model that lives in a very dark house where the light of day never penetrates the painted-black glass windows that are nailed shut to prevent the evil from escaping.

For bookings and contact info, visit her MM page at :
http://www.modelmayhem.com/lilialuster

Natalie Spaulding

Natalie is a freelance photographer based out of Hope Mills, NC. She was responsible for the pics in our Metal Massacre Mayhem magazine insert this issue, and more of her work will be featured in our next edition.

When not busy photographing nearly-nekkid women, Natalie can be found most days landscaping and hanging out at Sushi bars.

Joy Doe

Joy is the lady responsible for the beautiful landscape photography seen in our vampire snuff story this issue. While she is often mistaken for Michelle Rodriguez, they are two very different people. "Michelle often punches people or shoots them in her films," Joy explained. "In my films, I just stab people. Nothing beats a good shank to the skull."

Divinna Lynn

This Philly-born runway model just recently started doing model photography. As you can see from her pics in this issue, we think she has a very bright future ahead of her. Divinna lives in central NC and can be contacted through her MM page at:
http://www.modelmay hem.com/1059304

Seth Desjardins

Seth lives in Maine and is co-founder of AP&P Comics, who put out the best underground comix this side of R. Crumb and Grass Green. Buy some awesome reading material at **www.apandpcomics.com** and go nuts.

Dave and Will have just bombed an abortion clinic. Tomorrow, they're getting married.

William and David are homosexuals. They're also Born-Again Christians.

William and David are registered Republicans. Yet they drive a Prius.

William and David are straight-edge vegans. They also drink Malt Liquor.

William and David belong to PETA. But they both love genuine leather.

William and David oppose tobacco taxation. Still, they voted for Obama.

William and David believe in equal rights for all races. But they don't like dark - skinned people.

You see, Will and Dave are complex. Hard to pin down. Contradictory, even. Just like the flavors in their favorite snuff. Just like the articles in their favorite magazine.

Dave and Will are snuff takers.

The Ephemeris is their magazine.

Reserve your copy of The Snuff Taker's Ephemeris today at www.snuffmagazine.org.

THE VAMPIRE

A fool there was and he made his prayer

(Even as you and I!)

To a rag and a bone and a hank of hair

(We called her the woman who did not care),

But the fool he called her his lady fair

(Even as you and I!)

Oh the years we waste and the tears we waste

And the work of our head and hand,

Belong to the woman who did not know

(And now we know that she never could know)

And did not understand.

A fool there was and his goods he spent

(Even as you and I!)

Honor and faith and a sure intent

But a fool must follow his natural bent

(And it wasn't the least what the lady meant),

(Even as you and I!)

Oh the toil we lost and the spoil we lost

And the excellent things we planned,

Belong to the woman who didn't know why

(And now we know she never knew why)

And did not understand.

The fool we stripped to his foolish hide

(Even as you and I!)

Which she might have seen when she threw him aside--

(But it isn't on record the lady tried)

So some of him lived but the most of him died--

(Even as you and I!)

And it isn't the shame and it isn't the blame

That stings like a white hot brand.

It's coming to know that she never knew why

(Seeing at last she could never know why)

And never could understand.

- RK, 1897

This Issue Dedicated to Rudyard Kipling, 1865-1936.

NEWS
EXTRA STRONG
WHITE

SwedishSnus

07 EXTRA STRONG WHITE
06 EXTRA STR PORTION
05 STRONG W
02 STRONG PORTION
0 ORIGINAL PORTION

THE
LAB
SERIES

★★★
SWEDISH MATCH'

WARNING: This product can cause
gum disease and tooth loss.

Parting Shot

"Fresh air makes me throw up. I can't handle it. I'd rather be around three De Nobili cigars blowing in my face all night."

Frank Sinatra

STE presents:

MONSTER METAL
MEGAZINE

August 1987   2.99

Ultra-Hot Pixx Inside!

On The Couch With:

Motörhead

Mercyful Fate

GUNS N ROSES

SUBSCRIBE TO MMM NOW AND SAVE MONEY!

Just take it from Tommy, who suffers from a psychosis known as Perfect Pitch:

"Before this magazine came along, I would just sit in front of my piano or behind my guitar and noodle away endlessly. But then I started reading about snuff, and how it could focus my concentration. Well sir, I went out and bought the biggest bag of snuff I could afford from my friend JoJo, and let me tell you- it works!

Now I sit down at the piano and pump away for days, even though to me it just seems like minutes. Whenever I start feeling tired, I take another pinch of that awesome white snuff and just keep going! Sure, there's the occasional nosebleed and rampant paranoia, but what's to lose when you're making music that nobody else wants to hear! Thanks MMM!"

For **ALL** musicians & instruments!

Note From The Thrasher

Whoa Dudes and Dudettes! 1987 is shaping up to be an incredible year so far! Breakthrough albums by groups like Guns n' Roses and Carnivore are rocking us solidly, while new acts like Danzig (formerly of Misfits, Sam Hain) has just came out with his first solo album. That album features backing vocals from none other than Metallica's James Hatfield, who released the excellent *Garage Days Re-Released* EP featuring new bassist Jason Newstand.

In sad news, Twisted Sister has disbanded following the excellent *Love is for Suckers* album. I caught up with drummer Richie Teeter outside of the state park where he was camping with his family. I asked him a few questions about the breakup, but he was saying stuff like "who are you?" and "why are you bothering me while I'm on vacation with my family?" HA! Twisted Sister has always been known for their sense of humor and Richie is no exception.

Motörhead just came out with their new album *Rock n' Roll*, which is a masterpiece in metal music. Make sure you read more about it in our featured article.

Richie Teeter (Twisted Sister, left) hanging out with publisher Rockin' Ron Hubbard.

Also, Whitesnake just released their self-titled album. I don't know about you guys, but this thing has been on my turntable non-stop for the last two weeks! I don't ever see these guys just fading into obscurity in a few years.

And Ozzie has just come out with *Tribute*, a live album featuring a stunning performance by the now-deceased virtuoso guitarist Randy Travis. Former Kiss guitarist Ace Frehley has a new album out with his side project *Frehley's Comet*. While it looks like the rest of Kiss is losing a lot of listeners, Frehley seems like the kind of guy that will command a cult following for the next few decades, probably having his own TV show at some point and marrying a softcore porn actress. Keep on rockin', Ace!

The main question around the office this year has been "who rocks the hardest?" Thrash bands like Rush and Jethro Tull seem to be on the top of the list, but my pick is still Mötley Crue, whose *Girls, Girls, Girls* album actually shook the walls of my mom's basement so loudly that she thought it was Revelation times and the antichrist was coming! I also like the songs *Dancing on the Glass* and *Wild Side*, which are anti-drug ballads that so many bands nowadays are scared to talk about. Of all the best-selling rock groups out there, it's nice to know that you can count on Mötley Crue to be clean and sober and actually send a positive message to the 12 year olds that buy their albums.

Keep on Rockin'!

Rockin' Ron Hubbard

Letters

My mom says that the more I listen to Heavy Metal Music, the more demonic I'm becoming. I collect horror magazines, Masters of the Universe figures, and Dungeons and Dragons roleplaying games, and she sees these things as being satanic, and now she forbids me from keeping them in the house. What should I do?

Charles Edmund Cullen,
Hoboken, New Jersey

We suggest totally getting rid of everything your mother dislikes. They say that having positive releases and hobbies keep you from doing things like acting out homicidal tendencies, but we believe that's a bunch of malarkey. Get rid of your metal albums and take up a career in something that pays well, like the medical profession.

Dear MMM,

Thanks for continuing to send me your magazine even though I'm on death row. I'm not allowed to have a record player, so I have no way of knowing what's going on with my favorite bands. Keep rockin' hard!

Richard Ramirez
San Quentin, California

Thanks Richard! So many innocent people are on Death Row nowadays. We know that someone like yourself who listens to the same type of music that we do could in no way be responsible for whatever crime you've been falsely accused of. We hope that 25 years from now, you'll still be alive and subscribing to our magazine. God bless you.

Guys,

I've been listening to this really killer rock group out of Seattle called *Green River*. I'd like to know more about them and see them featured in a future issue.

Gary Ridgway,
Tacoma, Washington

Gary, we've been listening a lot to Green River's Come on Down EP *but we just don't see any of the band members going on to do better things. Besides, Seattle is never going to be a musical hotspot like LA or Chicago so you might as well stop listening to these guys. We heard they're on the verge of breaking up anyway.*

Dear MMM,

What's been going on with Pantera lately? I've been a huge fan ever since 1983's *Metal Magic* and I love their glam-rock and spandex-inspired stage costumes. (Their guitarist, Diamond Darrel, looks better in makeup than Lita Ford!)

Terrie Lee is an awesome singer, and can hit those high notes like nobody's business, not even King Diamond. But now I hear that they're thinking about selling out and becoming a "hard" rock band that won't do as much falsetto and instead be a kind of guttural sound like Slayer. Well, I say we don't need another Slayer. Pantera's just fine the way they are. If this new guy Phil Ensemble takes the band in a new direction, I'm sure their record sales will tank and they will break up shortly after.

Seth Desjardins,
Baton Rouge, Louisiana

Rock on Seth! Let's hope their next album isn't titled The Great Southern Bandwagon*!*

Rock News

- Slash, lead guitarist of GUNS N' ROSES, is thinking about giving up smoking. When asked when he plans to stop, he answered "probably in about **25** years, or whenever Camel starts making shitty snus."

- Dave Grohl, drummer for the band SCREAM, recently shared a dream he had with us. "It was a long time from now, and I was fronting a band called Food Fighters or something, and someone throws me a can of snus while I'm on stage, and I eat it." Sounds weird, Dave! He also mentioned spending a lot of time with Seattle band Nirvana, who are working with The Melvins drummer Dale Crover for a **12** song demo that may end up being an album called "Bleach" one day.

- Swedish death metal band Conquest is changing their name to Grotesque, with the addition of new singer Tomas Lindberg (aka Goatspell). However, Lindberg doesn't see much coming out of the project and so he says that he'll likely leave the group in the next year to pursue his own band, tentatively titled AT THE GATES. Then he gave us a can of General and we totally rocked out.

- Tony Iommi, the sole remaining original member of BLACK SABBATH, was recently caught chatting with Vivian Rose about the merits of Dean Swift snuff. Black Sabbath's new album "Eternal Idol" ships next week. (It sucks pretty bad, though).

- A new band out of Sweden is making waves for the extreme nature of their metal along with their prodigious snus use. Keep an eye out for MESHUGGAH, who despite their name are not Jewish.

- Now that King Diamond has struck out on his own after the critically acclaimed Mercyful Fate project has ended, we tracked him down in his nice Texas home, which is reportedly haunted. We asked him if now that he's left the comfy confines of his native Scandinavia, will he abandon Swedish snus for a more domestic brand, like Copenhagen or Happy Days? His only answer was "....AAAAAAAAABBBBBBIGGGGAAAAAAAAAAAAAAAAAAAAAAAIIIIILLLLLLL!"

BOO!!!

Oh No! AAAAHHHH!

LEFT: *King Diamond. He scares the hell out of Heather.*

Motörhead

Shuts Your Mouth

With a new snus from Swedish Match

(L-R): Phil Campbell, Lemmy Kilmister and Mikkey Dee. They know alchemy and they bring you Rock N' Roll. And Snus.

At a June 8th press conference, Motörhead announced their new joint venture with Swedish Match- a limited edition Motörhead snus!

Motörhead (by Grov) is limited to 150,000 cans worldwide so by the time you read this, it may already be gone. The flavor is a perfect blend of Ettan and Grov with that little bit of kick that you would expect from something with Motörhead's logo on it.

Mikkey Dee, the band's drummer (formerly with Mercyful Fate and King Diamond) is one of the greatest drummers in hard rock history. He also happens to be Swedish and a dyed-in-the-wool Grov fanatic. "I love snus and have been using Grovsnus as long as I can remember," he says, adding that several members of the road crew have been able to kick the cigarette habit by switching to snus.

"There are a million reasons not to smoke, one of which is that playing drums with both your hands occupied is a bit tricky!" he added.

But what about Lemmy? Will he ever kick his trademark three-pack-a-day Marlboro Red habit? "Maybe..." he said. "Maybe." (You can do it Lemmy!) "It's getting harder and harder to find places to smoke at now."

The press conference was a blast, with the band fielding questions from the audience and signing autographs for fans. Staff writer Crimson Paige told Lemmy as he signed her *Probot* record "I bought this album 'cause you were on it!" Lemmy, ever the joker, reached into his pocket and offered to give Paige her money back!

Enjoy the photos from the conference, and check out *The Ephemeris*'s own Divinna Lynn as she modeled backstage after the show. (This particular shoot was so hot that our cameras melted at one point...)

STE

LEFT: DIVINNA FINALLY GETS HER COPY OF THE ULTRA-RARE "ANGEL CITY & OTHER CITIES LIVE- 1916" PROMO CD SIGNED.

BELOW: MIKKEY DEE REPRESENTIN'.

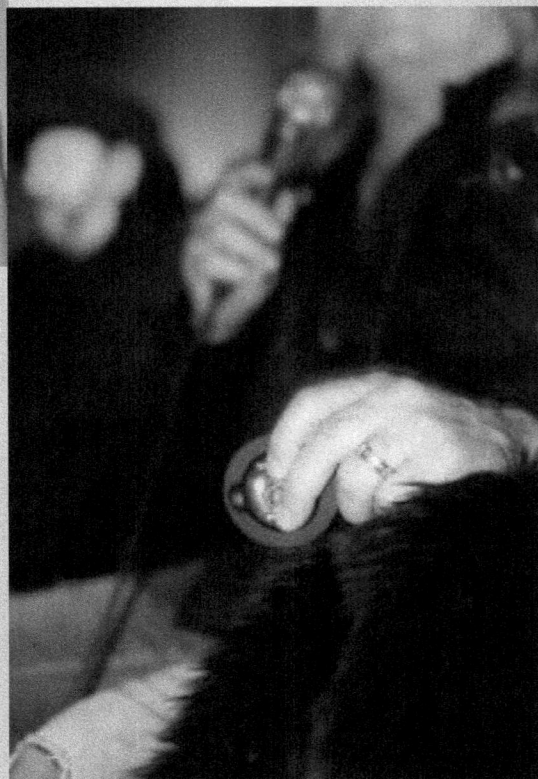

ABOVE: LEMMY: "WHY THE HELL IS THERE TWO LIDS?"

RIGHT: PHIL, LEMMY AND MIKKEY. FOR ALMOST 40 YEARS, THIS TRIO HAS PROVEN TO BE MOTÖRHEAD'D DEFINITIVE LINEUP.

Too Hot for Ingram Distibution

General Extra Strong or Motörhead by Grov? Decisions, decisions...

Our Favorite Motörhead Songs

We sat down with our staff and asked them to list their favorite Motörhead songs. If some of the song titles or album names seem unfamiliar to you, they're probably from Japanese bootlegs that you've never heard of yet. (But we have, because we're MMM). The same goes for the interview on the next page: the linotypist got the date wrong and put "2010" in place of "1987". WHOA! What was she smoking?

- **Jim Walter:** "1916"- Motörhead's answer to *Sky Pilot* or *Roland the Headless Thompson Gunner*. It's so appropriate that this is going to be in the Bela Lugosi issue, since that's the war he fought in, like the protagonist of the song. Thankfully though, Bela survived HIS wounds. I think the whole album was underrated personally.

- **Seth Desjardins:** When Rob asked me to name my "favorite" Motörhead song, I knew I couldn't just anoint one as a favorite. It would be equally as difficult to name a Motörhead song that I don't like. I like 'em all! A question I can answer is which Motörhead song comes to mind most often and that song is "Capricorn." I think the intro is great, it's got that sort of understated guitar bit in the beginning with the driving drums. Then you get Lemmy's growl in all it's glory.

The first time I heard this song was pretty early on in my experience with Motörhead. I had got a live collection and this song stood out. I just really enjoy the vibe and the lyrics; there's a sense of mysticism, but it's also a really personal song. The lyrics are actually a really good representation of the Capricorn character profile. Some particular passages that stand out include "Solitaire to the bone," and "When I was young I was already old." Capricorns are known to be solitary and also to have a sense of age about them in their youth (which interestingly enough seems to move towards youthfulness later in life).

Another lyric I love is, "They proved me right, they proved me wrong. But they can never last this long." This is also true of Capricorns who are known for their longevity and ability to persevere when others do not. And ... Who's lasted as long as Lemmy?! Not many. Kind of interesting when you think that he wrote this in the late 70's and he's still rocking to this day. I'm a Capricorn, just as Lemmy is so that naturally attracts me to this tune. [**Publisher's note: I didn't realize this until Seth pointed it out, but roughly half the staff of *The Ephemeris* are Capricorns, myself included. In fact, Bill Johnson, Larry Waters and me all share the same birthday- January 7th. Now you know why all of our articles are snarky, self-serving and arrogantly sarcastic. It's because we're so capricious.**]

A lot of people may think the guitar overdubs are a little too "out in the front" of the mix in the studio recording of Capricorn and I can see the merit in this point. I still love the song and although I don't remember the name of the live album I bought, I do prefer the live version. A very close second for Motörhead songs that most often come to mind has to be R.A.M.O.N.E.S. I mean, come on, a song about the Ramones that Lemmy wrote?! How cool is that?!

- **Mick Hellwig:** "Whorehouse Blues" - Even tough it's a recent song, it's so totally unlike Motörhead that I like it.

- **RW Hubbard:** "No Voices in the Sky" is the greatest Motörhead song from the greatest Motörhead album ever. When I first heard "Voices" on the radio I went out and bought the cassette the next day. Every song on that album should have been a number one hit.

- **Bill Johnson:** What's that one you played for me that had the horns? Where he says "intellectual heterosexual?" <u>Angel City</u>. I like that one.

- **David Thigpen:** "<u>I'm So Bad, Baby I Don't Care</u>." Why? 'Cause it's true.

- **Jennifer Goldsmith:** It's a toss up between "<u>Love Me Forever</u>" and "<u>Going to Brazil</u>", because they both remind me of high school and ex-boyfriends.

- **Crimson Paige:** "<u>Orgasmatron</u>," without a doubt. But every time I hear "<u>Stand by Me</u>", I break up in tears.

- **Micah Rimel:** "<u>Ace of Spades</u>." This song has a particular personal importance to me; in fact in changed my life, my persona and even my physiognomy. It's a dark and dangerous story, one I would have preferred be on the back-burners of my mind, but R.W. Hubbard demanded I tell the tale. He asked nicely and I refused. Then he asked not-so-nicely and put a gun to my head; a sweet little chromed out .32 Derringer. 'Nice gun'. I said, trying to mollify him. 'It is,' He responded with a laugh like the devil coughing up a chicken wing. 'Tell the story, Micah. Tell the $#%ing story!' He demanded; thrusting the gun so deeply in my ear I fancied it could hear my thoughts. So I thought of golden fried-chicken, delicious fried okra, homemade potato salad, watermelon so sweet it would melt your heart and collard greens steeped in lard. It worked. R.W. Hubbard got hungry and left me alone. This story is a true one, a sad one and a dangerous one. A story which nearly cost me my life at the shaky hands of a meth-addled sex-crazed donkey molester. Here goes:

It was a dark time in my life. I was running with the wrong crowd, smoking all the wrong substances, loitering at the wrong Taco Bell's. I was into Metal; bands like Crowbar, Pantera, Moonsorrow, Dimmu Borgir and Type-O-Negative. Then a 'friend' turned me onto Motörhead by playing "Ace of Spades". The devil was in me then. I grew muttonchops (a difficult task for anyone with American Indian genetics). I wore a biker jacket. I carried a gun. I only bought Magnum size condoms (my five kids can tell you how well those worked). I hung out in a biker bar called 'The Sandwiched Fresno Motor club and Health Spa'. It was really just a dive bar where you could get tanked on bathtub bourbon, grandma's old-timey crystal meth and then get a decent facial and mud-bath (little known fact; bikers LOVE to exfoliate. True story).

One day while partying away, Old Jimmy Fagbasher started chocking on a huge wiener (seriously, he loved his wieners) and I rushed over to save him. His face turned purple, then black, then purple again as I tried to apply the Heimlich. It wasn't working. I knew I had to do something drastic, so I screamed at the DJ, Senor Jose Finklestein, to play 'Ace of Spades'. The song pumped me up for what I knew I had to do. I punched the $#@& out of Jimmy. The wiener flew out of his toothless meth-mouth and his life was saved. He thanked me profusely and left me with two matching scars on my knees to remember him by before kicking me out of the club. He said my patchy black muttonchops were the only thing he could concentrate on whilst choking and thus keeping him alive.

I look back and sometimes miss those reckless days of violent depravity, but then I sober up and kick another stranger out of my bed and get on with my life. But, no matter what, I'll always have the "Ace of Spades."

[Authors Note: All the names, situations, events and circumstances have been changed, mutated and/or completely fabricated to protect the innocent.]

[Publisher's note: I can personally vouch for the validity of this entire memoir. Also, Motörhead just did a slow, acoustic version of "Ace of Spades" that you can find on youtube. It rocks my socks off.]

Mikkey Dee: The "Lost" Interview

Way back in 2010, staff writer Jim Walters calls us and says that the paper he works for gave him backstage passes for the Austin Motörhead show at Stubbs BBQ. We tell him to ask Mikkey Dee about a couple of snus rumors we've heard, especially the one about their own brand of snus. This is what was recorded. It was intended for inclusion in Volume One, but we didn't see the point, since it was so short. So here it is, finally.

JW: (March 26, 2010) I'm sitting backstage. The band did their last encore about 45 minutes ago. I haven't seen any of the Motorhead guys yet. I thought I saw Lemmy, but it was a roadie. After about an hour, Mikkey Dee walks buy with a towel around his shoulders and he's flanked by a couple of guys.)

JW: Mikkey! Have you got a sec for a couple of questions?

MD: Sure, what's up man?

JW: I'm doing an article about snus, and I saw in the documentary that you were using it.

MD. Hell yes! It's the best tobacco.

JW: What brands do you use?

MD: I like the natural flavors...

JW: Like Ettan?

MD: ...And Grov.

JW: (I start to ask him if there's any truth to the rumor that King Diamond uses snus, and someone hollers from back at the other end of the hallway.)

MD: Bruce! Oh shit, hold up a second.

JW: No problem, man. (Mikkey walks back into an area that I can't see. I hold for several seconds, actually about 45 minutes, but he never returns. I finally get tired of being eyed by a big bald fat guy with Buddy Holly glasses, so I walk out front where the drunk kids are still shouting "Lemmy!" and moshing in the dirt to pre-recorded tracks from *Motorizer*.)

I call it a night and head home.

Thunder

If the end is good, everything will be good

© v2 Snus, Denmark

Coming Next Issue:

OUR FIRST EVER HOLIDAY SPECIAL!

The Return of our Regular Features!

- JF Ljunglöf: King of Ettan
- Bill Johnson picks a bone with Altadis
- STE Hits the Radio
- Mr. Manners: Round Two
- 160 Years of Lucky Strike

...plus much, MUCH more!

Tentative street date: 12/7/12

STE®

www.ingramcontent.com/pod-product-compliance
Lightning Source LLC
Chambersburg PA
CBHW081655270326
41933CB00017B/3175